Memoirs
of
Ruth Hoffmann Johnson

Copyright © 8/1/2021 by George D. Dill

All rights reserved. No part of this book may be reproduced or transmitted in any form or by any means, electronic or mechanical, including photocopy, recording or any information storage or retrieval system without prior permission from the publisher.

First Edition

Submit comments and questions to georgeddillauthor.com

Paperback ISDN: 978-1-7379482-0-9

Let Ruth's life be remembered!

Ruth Hoffmann Johnson freely gave her gift of love to all she knew. When she was in the midst of her eighth decade of life, her daughter, Mary, suggested and encouraged Ruth to write her Memoirs. Ruth recognized that this would be an excellent way to continue giving her gift of love to her many descendants, especially those yet unborn as well as those of her friends. Let this book convey Ruth's great gift of love to each of you who read this book.

Contents

A Tribute to Ruth {ix}

Forward {xv}

Acknowledgments {xviii}

1
The Julius and Louisa Hoffmann Family {1}

2
The Agathon and Grace Hoffmann Family {7}

3
Mother Marries My Uncle Will {14}

4
Moving Closer to St. Louis and the Hoffmann Family {18}

5
My Mother Dies {20}

6
Living with My Uncle William's and Aunt Amelia's Family {26}

7
Serving as Governess of My Cousins {34}

8
Learning How Others Worked Through Their Troubles {37}

9
Moving on to Gallitzin, PA {41}

10
Living in Silver Lake Indiana {44}

11
Returning Home to St. Louis {48}

12
Learning a Marketable Trade {50}

13
Living With Mother and Father Koenitzer {55}

14
Learning the Sewing Business {65}

15
The Long Train Ride to California {70}

16
Determined to Earn My Own Way in Life {73}

17
Finding My First Paying Job and Room {75}

18
Using My Trade Skills and Enjoying Life in Pasadena, California {79}

19
Changing My Work – Becoming a Governess {83}

20
Finding New Inspirations at a Different Job in Los Angeles {85}

21
Time Out from Work to Be with My Dear Friend, Rhoda Mathews, in Her Time of Need {89}

22
Being a Children's Governess Again {97}

23
Rest and Recreation in Big Bear Mountains {105}

24
Back to Work: This Time at The Huntington Resort Hotel in Pasadena, CA {108}

25
Meeting and Marrying My "Prince Charming" Charles Stanley Johnson {112}

26
Meet Our First- Child – Ruth Francis {118}

27
Meet Our Second Child – Mary Louise {122}

28
Meet Our Third Child – Anita Louanne and Moving into Our Own Home {125}

29
The Blessings of Our Girl's Grandparents {131}

30
Life in My Own Home and Neighborhood {136}

31
My Three Girls Going to School – Kindergarten through Grade 4 {140}

32
My Three Girls Growing Up – Grades 5 Through 8 {148}

33
My Three Girls in High School – Grades 9 Through 12 {153}

34
Last Will and Testament of Mrs. Ruth Hoffmann Johnson {159}

35
Epilogue {163}

36
My Fond Memories of Grandma Ruth (GiGi) –
Cherished Moments Remembered by
Ruth's Grandchildren and Great Grandchildren {165}

37
Our Hoffmann-Morgan and Johnson-Lippincott Family Trees {183}

A Tribute to Ruth

With the publishing of this book, each of us in the Stanley Johnson-Ruth Hoffmann family want to proclaim a heartfelt tribute to you, *Ruth Hoffman Johnson*. This book not only contains your own testimony of how you lived your life, it also recalls some of the fond memories that we, some of your many descendants and friends have of you. You are lovingly admired and the joy your Memoirs brings to our lives inspires us to continue to fondly remember you.

"To you, Ruth, Mother, Grandmother, Great Grandmother (Gi Gi) and that which you taught each of us about how to live a purposeful and joy filled life will last forever".

Ruth lived a good long life of 94 years. As a young child, her life was abundantly filled by the love of her parents, grandparents and her many aunts, uncles, cousins and friends who lived in and near the city of St. Louis, Missouri. But she also endured a succession of tragedies with the death of her parents, her grandparents and her twin brothers, all within the first ten years of her life. Ruth persevered through those years of tragedy. In her teens and twenties, she learned the many life- and occupational-skills needed to make her own way in life while maintaining her faith in and love of God.

At the age of 32, Ruth's life blossomed. She met and married Charles Stanley Johnson, the one true love of her life. Together, they birthed and raised three beautiful daughters. Through the 35 years of their marriage, she lived a wonderful fulfilled life with her husband Stanley, and their three girls. They lived in their beautiful home which was situated at 1901 Euclid Avenue, San Marino, CA.

Figure 1 – Johnson Family Home Circa 1940

Ruth cherished each of her daughters as well as each of her grandchildren and great grandchildren. Perhaps part of the reason she loved and served her own family so much was because Ruth had lost the love of all of her birth family when she was so young. She did not want her own family to feel that loss of intimate mutual love among family members. Her love was also extended to her friends.

For nine years after all three daughters were married, Ruth and Stanley continued to enjoy the fruits of their own marriage together. Ruth made many home visits to each of her three married daughters and their growing families. A visit was most certain at the birth of each new grandchild. These visits were treasured times for Ruth as well as for each of her daughters and everyone in each of their families.

Yet again, tragedy struck with the death of her husband Stanley after 35 years of marriage. Once more Ruth needed to regather her love of life, leave her cherished home, move to an apartment and forge a new life for herself. She knew that she was mentally and physically able to be helpful to all of her family and friends. She would most definitely continue to love and cherish her three beautiful daughters and each of her grandchildren. She would also continue to meet and love each of her new grandchildren and even some great grandchildren who were yet to be born. For Ruth, there was still much for her to love and cherish in her long and purposeful life.

Given the suggestion plus a little coaxing from her daughter Mary, at the age of 83 and 84, Ruth wrote her memoirs. They are contained in two hand written "books". At the close of Book 2 of her hand written Memoirs, Ruth includes a holographic will. In it she laments, "I'm sorry that all didn't turn out as I had planned with the money. I wanted to at least leave each of my three daughters a thousand dollars apiece. But such did not turn out to be." Even so, the cherished memories Ruth left with each of her three daughters has far more value than said money. She most definitely left cherished loving memories within each of her daughters, each of her grandchildren, great grandchildren and each of her friends as well.

Through all of her life and especially so during the last 27 years her life, Ruth continued to share her love for her family via visits to the homes of each of her three daughters and each of her 13 grandchildren. She continued to send hand-written letters and make telephone calls to each of her daughters and their family. Although Ruth became frail in her last several years, she remained lucid and continued to love and encourage each of her family members throughout her long life. She left *"A Treasured Legacy"* within each of us who knew her.

Ruth's 94 years of life is *"A Treasured Legacy"* of a life well lived. She brought much love and joy to each of her family members and her many friends. Her greatest joys were home visits with her three girls and her many grandchildren. A treasured photograph taken at one of these joyful visits is shown in Figure 2.

Figure 2 – Ruth's Three Girls Bring their Families Home to Celebrate Ruth's 59th Birthday

The photograph in Figure 2 was taken in March 1954. Reading from left to right, front row center is Ruth and to her left is her grandson Hugh (Chip) Gordon. In the second row are Chuck and Mary Coppock, Anita Dill and Ruthie Gordon. George Dill is in the back row and Hugh Gordon was taking this photograph. Stanley is still at work and joined the family gathering later that evening.

The primary purpose of this book is to preserve the knowledge of the exemplary life that Ruth Hoffmann Johnson lived and told in her own hand written words nearly 40 years ago (written in 1983-84). By preserving her writings in this public book form, all of her progeny may acquire and read this book to learn of her many joys, trials and tribulations, of her great successes and sorrows and of her compassionate love for each one within her large family and her many friends. We are all beneficiaries of her widespread love and her well-lived life.

A secondary purpose of this book is to present an accurate four generation Hoffmann-Morgan Family Tree that Ruth began in her hand written Memoirs. In this book, Ruth's Family Tree begins with the birth of her great grandparents who were born at the end of the 18th century or beginning of the 19th century and continues to Ruth who was born at the end of the 19th century and her twin step-brothers who were born at the beginning of the 20th century – spanning a time of about 125 years. A similar family tree of the Johnson-Lippincott family tree is also presented in Chapter 37 for the convenience of Ruth's grandchildren and later generations.

Using modern computers and the Internet, Ruth's present and future progeny can now easily name their own parents, grandparents, great-grandparents, etc. back to one who is mentioned in these family trees, thereby continuing the connection of each family on through all future generations.

"When we read this book, we are filled with joy of the loving memories we have of you, Ruth Hoffmann Johnson. You left a plethora of treasured memories and possessions that were handed down to your grandchildren and great grandchildren who continue to encounter these possessions and photographs. Every encounter of your photographs and possessions brings back treasured memories of you. Moreover, you left your hand written Memoirs which are now published in this book so that an ever-growing number of descendants of your daughters as well as the descendants of your friend's families may read and rejoice over the legacy of the life you lived."

"Thank you, Ruth. May God's blessings be upon you and all of your families' descendants and your friend's descendants."

George D. Dill, Son-in-Law
Editor and Publisher

Forward

Ruth Hoffmann Johnson was born in 1895 and died in 1989. The time frame about which she wrote her Memoirs is limited to the first half of her life, the first half of the 20th Century. She personally wrote her Memoirs in long hand in 1983 and 1984 when she was 88 and 89 years old. In total, her hand-written version consists of two books, Book One of 36 pages and Book Two of 58 pages. A copy of these two handwritten books is preserved and may be read at the George D. Dill Family Library[1].

Many of the historic facts, photographs and memories presented here in this book would be lost forever without Ruth recalling her memories and thoughts about the many personal relationships she developed and cherished, the many trials and tribulations she experienced and overcame, the fine foods she cooked and shared, the many memorable places to which she traveled and lived and the ever-so-many delightful and tragic events she witnessed and recalled, personally going back over more than 80 years from when she wrote her Memoirs. We are all blessed immensely by this forthright, positive thinking, warm, loving and courageous woman, Ruth Hoffmann Johnson.

In order to keep the delightful flavor and intent of the author, it was decided to keep the text of this book just as it was written by Ruth in her hand written books even though some of the sentences are worded differently than we commonly speak today. Sometimes, Ruth, also interlaces a new memory when telling one of her old stories.

Whenever the name Ruth is used in this book, it is referring to Ruth Hoffmann in her younger years and to Ruth Hoffmann Johnson in her married life. Ruth's first daughter is fondly referred to as "Ruthie".

The historic and geographic information contained herein have been found accurate and true. The genealogical information presented by Ruth of her family has been expanded by locating and comparing the official government and genealogic documents available today via the Internet.

All through the first youthful years of her life, Ruth read and dutifully listened to her Grandfather Julius and her Uncle Will preach their sermons from the King James Bible. She actively continued to read and study the bible through the following 30 years of her life. She knew and understood the bible well and practiced its teachings all through her long life.

The reader of this book may note that Ruth knew and practiced well the precepts of the scriptures. Particularly notable by the Editor of this book is her adherence to the Christian Bible verses of 1 Peter 2:1-2, "So put aside all malice and all deceit and hypocrisy and envy and all slander. Like newborn infants, long for the pure spiritual milk, that by it you may grow up to salvation."[2]

Those of us who knew her well, knew that Ruth would not speak or write of others in a negative way. But having heard each of her stories many times over the nearly forty years that the Editor knew her, an insight was eventually gained into what really happened in each story and why it happened. For some of Ruth's stories, Editor's Notes have been added following her words to *"tell the rest of the story"*. The Editor's Notes are printed in smaller, italics font to distinguish them from Ruth's own hand written texts.

Footnotes are also used to make certain subjects clearer and give credit to the sources of some of Ruth's stories and photographs included herein.

---

1   You may make arrangements to view these and other documents and photographs referenced in this book at the George D. Dill Family Library by leaving a request at the following website; [georgeddillauthor.com].

2   Copied from the English Standard Version of the Christian Bible

Acknowledgments

It is most important to acknowledge the great contribution Ruth Hoffmann Johnson made to all of her family and friends, as well as to their descendants and others, in writing her Memoirs about the first half of her life.

Although the words of Ruth's Memoirs presented within this book can aid the reader to perceive the warm, loving and courageous woman Ruth was, they cannot capture the true depth of love she felt and freely expressed for each member of her family and each friend. "Thank you, Ruth for your gift of love to each of us who knew you. Thank you for writing this book. It brings back to life our fond memories of you."

We also owe our heartfelt thanks to you for many other obvious reasons. "Thank you, Ruth!", for taking the responsibility at the early age of eight to begin preserving the many important family documents, photographs, newspaper clippings of your family, friends and acquaintances plus mementos of many memorable events you were part of throughout your long life. "We cherish all that were found. A copy of some is included herein."

"Thank you, Ruth!", for the many items you specifically preserved within your "Birch Bark Scrapbook" for this express purpose, to graphically add more to your story for all of your descendants and others to see things as they were in your time. You also consciously preserved special photographs of your family and friends in your several photo albums. You also left us your "Metal Box" of personal documents and photographs.

After Ruth's death, many of the cherished items Ruth preserved, found their way into the possession of her three girls and then to her grandchildren. A search was made among her many family descendants to find and take photographs of each item referenced in her two handwritten books containing her Memoirs. The photographs of those items found are included in this book alongside her reference to that item. Some additional photographs of people, places and things were found and included with appropriate notes to provide Ruth's descendants and others who read this book a better visual picture of what Ruth saw and experienced when she was living these events about eighty or more years ago.

We all owe a special "Thank You!" to Mary Louise Johnson Coppock, Ruth's second daughter, and her husband Chuck, for the loving care they gave Ruth during the later years of Ruth's life. Mary is also the one who suggested that her mother write her Memoirs and continued to encourage her mother while she was writing. Without Mary's generous contributions and loving guidance during the later years of Ruth's long life, these historical facts and memories of Ruth's life would not exist.

Shortly after Ruth's death, her three daughters, Ruth Francis Johnson Gordon (Ruthie), Mary Louise Johnson Coppock and Anita Louanne Johnson Dill gathered to execute their mother's will. They unanimously agreed to follow Ruth's last wishes as expressed in the final six pages of Book 2 of her hand written Memoirs. It was further decided that the original hand written manuscripts of both Book 1 and Book 2, *"Memoir of Ruth Hoffmann Johnson"*, would be held for safe keeping by Ruth Francis Johnson Gordon (Ruthie"), the first daughter of Ruth, who lived in New Zealand. This momentous decision preserved the primary purpose of the time, love and effort that Ruth spent writing her Memoirs.

We owe a special "Thank You!" to Anita Louanne Johnson

Dill, Ruth's third daughter, for recognizing the historic and genealogical value of her mother's Memoirs. Anita made seven copies of the two hand-written manuscripts that day, one copy for each of her four children and one copy for each of Marry Coppock's three children. Ruthie would make copies, one for each of her six children from the original copies that she held. Making and distributing copies of Ruth's Memoirs was an important second step in preserving this historic and genealogical information. It also enabled making this information available to all oncoming generations of Ruth's descendants via this book.

Thirty some years after Ruth Hoffmann Johnson's death and the distribution of the handwritten copies of Ruth's Memoirs, George D. Dill, third son-in-law of Ruth and Stanley Johnson and Editor of this book, became interested in researching his children's genealogy, one-half of which were the ancestors of the Stanley Johnson and Ruth Hoffmann families. Upon making some progress in this new project via the Internet and showing the results to his son, James K. Dill, Jim reminded his father of the two hand-written books titled, *"Memoir of Ruth Hoffmann Johnson"* and mailed a copy to his father. The Hoffmann family names and dates presented in these two hand-written books were very helpful in accurately piecing together four generations of the Hoffmann-Morgan family genealogy.

We also owe Ruth yet more thanks for preserving other family documents and mementos. Upon reading Ruth's Memoirs, the Editor also remembered that, during one of her many visits some 60 plus years before, Ruth had given him four pages copied out of the Johnson-Lippincott family tree plus two pages of the Hoffmann-Morgan family. These pages of the Johnson-Lippincott family trees provided authentic given names of several generations of the Johnson-Lippincott ancestors in appropriate relationships within each family. These unique given names were needed to verify which of the many Johnson and Lippincott families in New Jersey, the Hoffmann and Morgan family lines who had lived in Germany and Whales during the 19th century were our true family ancestors.

In 1970, Ruth planned a two week visit to the Dill family home in Gaithersburg, MD. The primarily purpose was to visit with her third daughter Anita Dill and her husband and their four children. Knowing that her daughter and family now lived in Maryland and checking a map, Ruth found that she would only be 40 miles from where she lived in Hagerstown, MD some sixty years prior. Upon arriving at the Dill family home, Ruth suggested that it would be great if she and the entire Dill family could tour the town of Hagerstown since it was relatively close to the Dill family home. A plan was soon set; we made it an all-day family tour so all of the family could hear the stories Ruth had to tell about her life in the town of Hagerstown, MD some sixty years before our visit.

On the first weekend of that particular visit, all of the Dill family (George, Anita, Karen, Lisa, James and George Charles) and Ruth climbed into their large Town and Country Ford station wagon. Since the distance between their home and Hagerstown was only 41 miles, the travel time was just a little over one hour when we added a short stop at a special creamery store in Middletown, MD called "Main Cup" to get ice cream cones for everyone.

Ruth was enthused and excited to see Hagerstown again. She recognized the brick town house with iron railings where she lived. She was happy to see downtown Potomac Street again and the large homes with terraced flower gardens up on the small hill farther up Potomac Street. As we drove slowly around the four-block square of the downtown streets and up Potomac Street, Ruth was recalling many of her memories, like knowing the Holzapfel and Himmel families and where they each lived, recalling how good the pretzels tasted at the Himmel's saloon, etc. (see Chapter 6). To see and hear Ruth's excitement and hear the memories pour out was a great memorable experience for each of us present on that tour.

We owe a "Thank you!" to Karen Alexander for helping her grandmother Ruth record some of her memories of life in Hagerstown, MD on a small tape recorder some years after the Dill family visit to Hagerstown.

We owe a "Thank You!" to Dianna Gordon for taking charge and preserving the original manuscripts of Ruth's two-volume, handwritten Memoir plus the remaining contents of her "Birch Bark Scrapbook". Dianna also made copies of photographs she had saved out of Ruth scrapbooks. Copies of several of these photographs are included in this book.

I, the Editor, want to offer my heartfelt "Thank you!" to Carole R. Dill and James K. Dill for their great assistance in the proof reading and editing of the several drafts that became this final manuscript as well as their personal encouragement and support through the two-year long process that was needed to produce this book. Also, I greatly appreciate the suggestions, guidance and support that both Carole and James offered towards the formatting, editing and production of this book.

I also want to thank Christopher Coppock for his personal support and the use of his e-mail to speed up the communication of photographs and documents between Mary Coppock and me.

The Editor also wants to thank our distant cousins, who are members of the Hoffmann and Morgan families, he met virtually via the Internet during his search for family and genealogical documents available on the Internet. Their contributions, thoughts and encouragement are much appreciated. In particular he offers his thanks to two of Ruth's distant cousins, Lori Mellies and Bud Pickett, who were most helpful in finding and providing information about Ruth's paternal grandfather, the Rev. Julius Hoffmann. The editor also wants to thank Margaret Scudds who was helpful in finding information about Ruth's maternal grandparent, Elizabeth Morgan and her parents.

Now, with the publication of this book, ***the Memories of Ruth Hoffmann Johnson*** will always be available for all of our families. It is hoped that this book will be read by most if not all of the following generations of Ruth's descendants and they too will show and tell of the many stories contained herein to their children. It is also hoped that this book will be available to the descendants of Ruth's many friends mentioned in this book and their descendants.

All of us can rejoice in the overall message of this book, namely, Ruth's love-of-life, her love of God and fellow man and being forthright and proper with all whom she met.

Ruth Hoffmann Johnson's Memoir is not forgotten!

Rejoice in learning of the kindred spirit of Ruth!

May God bless each of you who read this book!

1

The Julius and Louisa Hoffmann Family

Grandfather: Julius Hoffmann, born in 1833.
Grandmother Sophia Louisa Kemmerich: no birthdate.
Both born in Germany.[3]

G randfather, a minister, was pastor of the Evangelical Lutheran Church in Caledonia, Racine County, Wisconsin where his son, Agathon, was born on October 29, 1869. Later in 1884 grandfather, Julius Hoffmann, was pastor of the evangelical St. Paul's Church in Mather's Creek, St. Louis County, MO.

Figure 3 - Julius J. Hoffman Circa 1885

Editor's Notes: The Editor used the Family Search and Ancestry websites along with other family members and searched selected archives to collect vital information and photographs for Ruth's Hoffmann-Morgan and Johnson-Lippincott family trees (See Chapter 37 of this book.). Except for Ruth's paternal grandfather's country of birth, all of her writings are proven to be accurate. No photographs of her grandparents were found in her possessions. The photograph in Figure 3 above was found in the archives of one of the churches in which Julius Hoffmann served. It is believed to be taken circa 1885.

Grandfather and Grandmother were parents of thirteen children, four of them passing on at an early age. The names of their nine remaining long living children were as follows:

Five Sons:	Four Daughters:
Daniel	Elizabeth
Paul	Mary
Charles	Margaret
Agathon	Louise
William	

1. Daniel – no family and never wed as far as I know. He was an engineer with the Cudahy Packing Company for years in Milwaukee, WI.
2. Paul – no information on him, he was a wanderer. As an uncle, I remember as a child liking him very much, the few times I saw him.
3. Charles – a minister, wife Minna. They had several children; Anna, the oldest is the only one that I know. We only saw each other a few times as children. Later in touch and we still correspond now in 1983. Her husband, Ray Gelsthorpe, a retired banker from Lincoln, IL where they lived before moving to Port Charlotte, Florida.
4. Agathon – a doctor, wife Grace – one daughter, Ruth (the au-

thor) – more later.
5. William – a Lutheran Minister was married three times. His first two wives and three children having passed on, he later married Amelia Toth, a daughter of one of his parishioners in Mt. Pleasant, IL. He and Aunt Amelia had fourteen children. I only knew seven of them: William, the oldest; Charles, Harold, Dorothy, Esther, Paul and Lester, the youngest. Paul, a widower with a family, lives in La Mesa, CA and Lester, with wife Shirley, lives in San Diego, CA. Lester is a superintendent of a school there.
6. Margaret – husband Theodore Meitz connected with a shoe company in St. Louis, MO. Two daughters, Martha and Hildegard.
7. Mary – husband, George Bleibtreu (stay true in English). They shortened their name later to True. Uncle George, a minister had three children, Samuel, John, and Hannah before they were married. Aunt Mary had three of her own, Daniel, Walter and George. Walter and his wife Laura lived in Beverly Hills, CA.
8. Louise – husband, Louis Jurgens who was in the grocery business. They had three children, Wilber, Mildred and one other son who was a minister. He passed on while still a young man.
9. Elizabeth – husband Charles Mellies, a doctor (homeopathic) and three children, Olga, who passed on as a small child, Almira and Walter. Walter, a fine musician. At one time he had an orchestra that played on the excursion boats on the Mississippi. He finally went through medical college and became a doctor like his father.

Three of the sisters, Elizabeth, Louise and Margaret and their families always lived in St. Louis. It was home base for all of the

Hoffmann family, no matter where they moved or traveled – always returning sooner or later for a visit. We had many happy get togethers through the early years and a birthday never was missed. It was always a fun time for all playing games etc. in those days.[4]

Aunt Elizabeth's was my favorite home to visit. She and Uncle Charlie always so welcoming and hospitable and I was there often. The house so big and roomy – and oh, those feather beds, – how cozy. They lived across the street from Hyde Park where one could watch the skaters on the pond in the winter from an upstairs window. Almira, a few years older was like a big sister to me – making cloths for my dolls (she had a small sewing machine) and giving me her books to read that she had finished earlier.

Figure 4 – Forrest Park, St. Louis, MO – copied from Wikipedia File

Walter also was lots of fun. He loved to play the piano being a musician at heart. He and I sat many a time at the piano singing, *"Meet Me in St. Louie, Louie, Meet Me at the Fair"*. That was the year of the St. Louis Fair in 1904, correctly named, *"The Louisiana Purchase Exposition"*. I was then nine years old and I spent that summer at Aunt Elizabeth's. That was the year after my mother passed away.

In the mornings, I attended German school – the rest of the

day in play or whatever the family was doing. We visited relatives on occasion and the Fair two or three times. That was fun, especially on the roller coaster and fun things.

Uncle Charlie often took us for a drive in the family car on Sunday afternoons. He also had a smaller car – I think it was called "The Tin Lizzy" at that time. He used it to call on patients in the afternoon as was the custom in those days; patients who were not able to come to the office. He often took me with him which was great fun. Uncle Charlie was such a kind, easy-going person; a pleasure to be with.

Figure 5 – 1904 Tin Lizzy – copied from Wikipedia File

At home, he often hid treats for us in the bag of a big cardboard Santa in the downstairs hall closet across from his office. It and his waiting room were in the home on the first floor – left side of the house with an outdoor entrance where patients could leave if they wished. Also, Uncle Charlie always kept a lively parrot in a cage in the waiting room to amuse the patients.

Aunt Elizabeth was a good soul, often visiting orphan's homes, taking gifts and treats for them. I remember well going with her a couple of times. Aunt Elizabeth, with the help of a maid, always kept their home shinning bright and being a good cook set a very delectable table. She cooked and canned many things that are bought ready prepared at the stores these days. She made her own sauerkraut and put-up green beans in the same way, in a huge crock. She also made the best sausage you ever tasted, put up in casings in link form, hung up on a rod in the basement for winter use. Aunt Elizabeth also made apple butter, the best ever, cooked in a large iron kettle in the back yard and that in the city. She always made plenty so they, being good active church members, donated much of it to the church for the fall Bazar.

Aunt Margaret and Uncle Theodore with their two daughters, Hildegarde and Martha, lived on Linton Ave. in St. Louis, several blocks from Aunt Elizabeth in a two-story house. Grandma Hoffmann and Aunt Lou, the youngest daughter and not yet married, lived upstairs. When in St. Louis, I spent a weekend there occasionally. Hildegarde and I, being the same age, were good friends – Martha, older. When in our teens, Hildegarde and her boyfriend, Fred Fix, would walk me part way home from church. She later married him.

---

3 More generations and details of the genealogy information of the Hoffmann-Morgan families are provided in Chapter 37 of this book.

4 The reader needs to realize that there were no movies, radios, TV's, cell phones, computers or Internet in the last half of the 1800s. Movies and radios were not readily available to the average family until the third decade of the 20th century. Daily TV programs became available to all in the mid-1950s.

5 Forest Park of St. Louis is one of USA's large (1,326 acres) urban public parks. Ruth mistakenly called it Hyde Park in her hand written memoirs. Hyde Park is the name of the community in St. Louis where some of her aunts and uncles lived.

2

The Agathon and Grace Hoffmann Family

The story of Ruth's birth and early childhood to age 4
1894 to 1899 – Mt. Olive and Mt. Pleasant, IL

As a young man, my father, Agathon Hoffmann, studied to become a homeopathic doctor[6] like his Uncle Charlie. While an intern in a hospital in Rochester, NY, he became acquainted with a Grace Morgan who had emigrated from Whales. I'm not sure but judging from the pictures from her album, all nurses, I think she also was a nurse.[7] However, she and my father fell in love and were married in Rochester, NY on February 19, 1894. I have their marriage license certificate.[8] (No marriage certificate found)

Editor's Notes: At the time of Ruth's death, no one within her family knew who was the subject of the many photographs that were in her photograph albums and steel box. Ruth's three daughters and all of her grandchildren had never met their maternal grandparents and many of

Ruth's friends who lived in the early part of the 20th century. We now know that the two photographs in Figure 6 below are of Agathon Hoffmann and Grace Morgan. It is believed that this photograph of Grace was taken on their wedding day and the one of Agathon was taken in St. Louis in 1894, soon after they were married and had returned to St. Louis. These two photographs were found in Ruth's steel box some 30 years after her death.

Figure 6 – Agathon and Grace (Bathsheba) Hoffmann

After my father graduated from medical college and was living on his own, they settled in Mt. Olive, Ill where I, Ruth, was born, March 30, 1895 – Later living in East St. Louis, when I was about four years old, my father became ill with typhoid fever. He was taken care of by Uncle Charlie Mellies in his home but never recovered. His passing was a sad happening for the whole family, I was told later. They all loved him so. Aunt Elizabeth had one of his letters she treasured and was going to leave it to me but I never received it.

I remember my father well as a very gentle soul. He named my first two big dolls – one Mary Christmas and the other Clementine Eugenie Antoinette. Sorry I didn't keep them.

I also had a pet chicken he named Stinker. We found it floating in the back yard one morning.

Figure 7 – Ruth Hoffmann at Age 3

Editor's Notes: Ruth was happy to tell her story about her pet chicken. "Sometimes my father would take me out into the back yard to see her pet chicken and all the hens. Stinker, my pet chicken, would come up to me and eat ground corn right out of my hand. I remember telling my father, 'Stinker did not have good manners because he made the ground corn go flying in all directions when he pecks at it in my hand'."

Sometimes Ruth would reminisce about the stories she had heard about her father – "... that he was a very loving person. My father was a true believer of the Gospel Message presented in the bible. He would tell others that he had God's calling to be a doctor and help others to be well both physically and mentally". Ruth sometimes concluded that this was probably why her father had to also work as a grocery store clerk because some of his patients that he doctored could not pay what was due for his services but he would still offer his services to them as needed.

Ruth would sometimes tell us how happy her father and mother were when they were together. "Often my parents and I would take a walk around the little town in which we lived. Sometimes. when I was holding their hands, they would swing me up into the air. I would squeal with joy and they would do it again. Sometimes I would run ahead and look back to see them holding hands, watching me and talking all the while. It was wonderful for me to experience and feel the warm love of both my mother and father. It was even more wonderful to observe and feel the love my father and mother had for one another."

Ruth often told the story about how she would greet her father when he was coming back from the grocery store. "On many days, my mother would ask me to go to the window in the living room to watch for my father and tell her if he was coming down the street. When I saw him, I would yell, 'He's coming!' and my mother would come running into the living room and we would wait just inside the door to greet him immediately when he opened the door. My father would pick me up, give me a big hug and kiss and while still holding me in one arm, he would put his other arm around my mother, give her a hug and kiss and we would all be one big hug together." These childhood years were remembered and recalled as very happy times for Ruth.

There was much flooding in East St. Louis at that time, which I think was the cause of so much typhoid fever, etc. and the cause of my father's death. I'm very thankful to have something of my father's – his medical certificate (see Attachment 1), his pen and a copy book of songs.[9] (His pen and book of songs were not found.)

My mother's *given* name was Bathsheba, but she didn't like it so had it changed to Grace – Grace Morgan.

Back to St. Louis – Besides the flooding in that part of the country, there was a depression at that time. My father was not able to collect his dues as a doctor so ended up working in Beacon's Grocery store and then he became ill and died in September 1899. I can still picture the store and area where we lived and remember our good neighbor, Mrs. Draper, who made me two pretty summer dresses – one white and the other deep blue.

Editor's Notes: Ruth recalled the day her father became sick. "I was just over four and one-half years old. I knew it was serious because my father not only looked bad but that morning my mother rushed to get herself and me ready to take my father to St. Louis on the street car. My mother said we were going to see my grandmother. Actually, we were rushing off to St. Louis to see my Uncle Charlie who was a homeopathic doctor".

"I loved going to Grandmother's home on the street car. During all the other times we took the street car to Grandmother's home, my father would sit with me and we would look for all the animals we could see out the window. But this time, he was leaning on my mother's shoulder with his eyes closed. When we were crossing the Ead's Bridge, he did not even open his eyes when I asked him to look at all the ships going up and down the Mississippi River. It took more than one hour to get there. I will never forget that day. It seemed like an awfully long time."

"When I entered the kitchen early one morning while we were at my grandmother's home, mother called me over to her chair and my grandmother came over as well. Mother said that she had something important to tell me. Looking right into my eyes, my mother said, 'Your

father passed away last night. He will not be coming back. Do you remember when Grandfather Julius passed away a few months ago. We have not seen Grandfather Julius since then and we will not be seeing your father again. Your father died peacefully last night and he is now with Jesus in heaven'. This was one of the wort moments in my life."

Ruth said she repeated the last two sentences her mother had just told her, that her father had gone to heaven and was not coming back. *"I was already missing my father. He was not going to be coming home again. I was not going to see my father again, ever. I did not want to hear this, so, I ran back to my bed and cried; I already missed my father so. In a while my mother came in and sat down next to me. My mother held me close in her arms. I began to sob. We both fell back onto the bed, holding each other and cried until I fell asleep."*

Ruth also recalled how she felt after the funeral services, *"My mother wasn't her happy outgoing self. She said, 'My true love has died. My heart is broken. My zest for life is gone.' My mother seemed not to know what to do each day. She was just here letting time pass. I tried some of my regular ways to get my mother's attention and make her laugh but they did not work this time."*

"No matter how many aunts and uncles came by to talk to my mother and to cheer both of us up, we both remained very sad for what seemed to be a long, long, long time."

Although Ruth was young when her father died (4 years and 8 months old), she often noted in our normal conversations that she had many happy loving memories of her mother and father during those early years of her life. To Ruth, it seemed her parents had a happy loving relationship and did most everything together with her. Ruth sometimes recalled that her mother would often sing some of her happy Welch songs while she was cooking dinner. Then Ruth would add with a big smile, *"Sometime while my mother was singing a song, she would pick me up and twirl around there in the kitchen between her stirring one pot and then another."*

My Mother and I moved back to St. Louis to live with my grandmother. Later I went to live with Aunt Elizabeth and Uncle Charlie to recuperate from this great loss.

In these early years, many a happy street car rides I had to St. Louis over the well-known Eads Bridge. Seeing all the boats and steamers going up and down the Mississippi was quite a romantic sight for a 3 and 4-year-old child, especially at night when many of the boats were lighted up.

Figure 8 – Ead's Bridge Over Mississippi River, From St. Louis, MO and East St. Louis, IL, copied from Wikipedia

---

6   See Attachment 1 – Photograph of Agathon Hoffmann's Dr. of Medicine Certificate.

7   Photographs of other graduates from Barnardo's School for Girls have been found wearing the same coat design. The coat that Ruth refers to is the standard suit provided by the Dr. Bernardo's School for Girls to all graduates of the school.

8   An extensive search was made for the original marriage certificate among Ruth's possessions now distributed among her grandchildren but it was not found.

9   A search was made for Agathon's pen and copy of songs but none were found. Being of this modern age, Ruth's grandchildren would not recognize what an old-fashioned pen would look like and they would not recognize the old songs so these things were most likely thrown away.

3

Mother Marries My Uncle Will

Ruth living with her Uncle Will – Age 6 to 7
1901 to 1902 – Ironwood, MI

About two years after my father passed on, my mother married my father's younger brother, William Hoffmann (Uncle Will), a minister. I didn't realize until we moved into a home of our own on Arco Avenue in St. Louis that I had a new father (step father). I was 6 years old and I had just started school, 1st grade.

Editor's Notes: Ruth sometimes recalled other things that happened months after losing her father. One of those she noted, "While my mother was still grieving the loss of my father, I noticed that all of my aunts and uncle were coming by to have serious talks with my mother and grandmother but I did not really understand what was happening then within my extended family. They would always send me out to play with one of my cousins and talk for hours before they finally left. Whenever I came into the room, all the talking would stop. I now realize that they were trying to convince my mother to marry my Uncle William. He was a young pastor. In those days a young pastor needed a wife to be accepted by a church. His former wife had died in child birth and so he needed to find a new wife. My mother was now a single Mom. She was an emigrant from Whales. She needed a husband to take care of her and her daughter. Even though my mother was not in love with my Uncle William, my extended family convinced my mother that she should marry my Uncle Will. They told her it would be good for her; it would be good for me and it would be good for Uncle William. This was a marriage of convenience, not love."

At another time, Ruth noted, "One evening my mother called me into the bedroom and told me that tomorrow there was going to be a wedding at Aunt Elizabeth's home. She was going to marry Uncle William and he would be my new stepfather. This was a shock to me. It was the first I had heard of the plan. It was to be a small family wedding. Only the Hoffmann family was invited. I was to put on my Sunday, go to church dress. My Uncle Charles Hoffmann, being a pastor, would preside over the wedding. And that evening my mother and I would move all of our things into the new apartment that Uncle William had rented for all of us to live in together. It seemed odd to me that even though weddings were always happy occasions, no one seemed to be happy about this wedding. There was not even a family celebration right after the wedding."

We lived 2 blocks from Forest Park where later in 1904 the St. Louis World's Fair was held. Being a very large park, there was a wonderful zoo with all the unusual animals we see today and many fun things to ride on. Earlier, we lived in another area on the King's Highway side. My little next-door neighbor and friend, Rosie, and I would wheel our doll buggies up to the park and play around the fir trees. Wonder if Rosie ever remembered later.

We moved from St. Louis, to Ironwood, Michigan. It was so cold and the snow so deep we couldn't even open our front door one morning. The ore dumps were great to slide down when we could make it. The spring and summer there were beautiful. I remember the cherry trees blooming in our back yard.

During the week, my mother would take care of things in the house and cook for our family while Uncle Will was preparing for his Sunday sermon. But mother was not her normal happy and enthusiastic self. It seemed like all the fun things in her life had gone away. No matter how hard I tried, things were not happy as they once were when my father was living.

My first school was only one block from home. We sat 2 in a seat in our room, 2nd grade. There was one little negro girl in the class. Her name was Tillie but no one would sit with her. I think it was because the children there were not use to black people. Having come from St. Louis and being use to them, Tillie sat with me. She was fun, use to dip her braids in the ink well. She and I always beat the others in class, climbing up the poles in the play yard for our exercise class.

Our new school, some blocks away and built on the edge of town, had white pillars and always reminded me of the White House in Wash., DC. It was a two-story building. Lovely country side beyond and a woody strip just a few steps away that I was reminded of when watching some of the Walt Disney pictures. Real lush and green with violets, lady slippers, John-in-the-pulpits, and many more wild flowers growing around old tree stumps. There were also buttercups and pussy-willows growing along the stream which ran under the boardwalk part way out into the country where parishioners of my uncle's church lived. They, I believe, were farmers. They had the first underground cellar I had ever seen where they stored their vegetables, etc., for the winter.

Back to school for a minute – Almost forgot my art class there. Though I am far from being an artist, I remember enjoying making calendars there in class – can still see the room. We must have had a very good teacher. The only name I remember from Ironwood is Milky. They had a shop across from the railway station and were members of my uncle's church.

While in Ironwood, my uncle served as pastor at a second church in Bessemer some miles away. The only thing that I remember from there is staying in a parishioner's home over night and sleeping on the floor on a mattress well covered and tucked in but somehow in my sleep got my head down where my feet belonged and yelling for help. It came.

4

Moving Closer to St. Louis and the Hoffmann Family

Our family moves closer to St. Louis – Age 7 to 8
1902 to 1903 – Mt. Pulaski, IL

From Ironwood, we moved to Mount Pulaski, Ill. Ministers, it seems, moved often in those days, at least my uncle did. My little friends in Ironwood envied me to be moving near St. Louis where I might see the St. Louis Fair. Even in the earlier years, such affairs were well advertised far in advance it seems.

We lived in the parsonage next to the church in Mt. Pulaski. It was a very nice town with a 4-block square in the center of town. In the center of the square was the post office building with perhaps other offices. On one corner I think was a canon and the building, come to think of it, that housed the post office was the court house. All the shops were in 3 blocks facing the front and sides of the square – homes in the rear. On one corner was sort of a family hotel where Abraham Lincoln stayed at one time. My Uncle had a piece of wood from the room he occupied hoping to have a cane made of it. Some of Abraham Lincoln's descendants lived around the corner from our church.

In the square block on the corner lived the Roth's, members of our church. Margarite the youngest daughter and I were good friends being about the same age. Many a happy hour we spent together under lovely fruit trees, wonderful plums, peaches, etc. We also went to a school together. Margarite was in 2nd grade, I being a bit older was put in 3rd grade. Wanting to be in Margarite's class, I made the mistake of pretending to be asleep when called upon in class so was demoted to 2nd grade. I loved school there, especially the play yard at that age. One cute little boy, Webster Perveance, always played with the girls at recess time. Names I remember of friends there were, Tiny Spitler, Doris Gruber, Gretchen Figenhour and Fern Drobisch. We all had so much fun together. These are times one doesn't forget.

5

My Mother Dies

My Mother's Death – Age 8 to 9
1903 to 1904 – Mt. Pulaski, IL

Life wasn't all happiness for us in Mt. Pulaski. My mother and I were as close as any mother and child could be. We often took walks in the evening and I knew she wasn't very happy for she often wept when we were out. I had no idea what was wrong or that she wasn't feeling well.

Editor's Notes: Ruth did reveal that the daily life of her mother and Uncle Will was not like the daily life that her mother and father enjoyed. Her Mother and Uncle Will were sometimes at odds with one another. Ruth said, she could see that her mother was trying to make this a good marriage so that she and I would have a good family life. Ruth also tried to not be a bother to her Uncle Will so that he would be happy for her mother. But it was obvious to Ruth that their marriage was one of convenience, not out of true love. When things were really bad, her mother would get their coats and they would take a walk. Ruth once said, "There was nothing I could do except hold my mother's hand

and love her."

One evening I was sent across town for the doctor – no telephone in those days. That same evening, I was invited to spend the night with a good neighbor. In the morning she told me that my mother had passed on and that I had 2 new baby brothers – twins – all of this happened on 21st December, 1903.[10] She also praised my mother, telling me what a good and helpful person she had been and well loved by all. In her own words, "She would have given the shirt off her back to help anyone." I remember her words well.

Editor's Notes: Ruth was eight years old when her mother died. When they told her that her mother had passed away, Ruth said she immediately understood what that meant. She had already experienced the death of her beloved grandfather and her wonderful loving father just four years prior. She still missed them. Now her mother was gone. Ruth expressed her first thoughts, "What will happen to me? What will happen to my twin baby brothers?"

For weeks Ruth was very confused about the depth and breadth of emotions she was having. She was heartbroken that her mother was gone but she was happy that she had her baby brothers to care for. Her Aunt Louise had come to take care of Ruth and her twin brothers. And each day her Aunt Louise was teaching Ruth how to hold a baby, how to feed and burp a baby and how to change a baby's diaper so that she could help take care of her twin brothers. This was exciting for Ruth. It took her mind away from the loss of her mother.

Ruth was also anxious about what was going to happen to her and her brothers. They had no mother now. They had no family of their own. In time, Ruth began hoping that one of her extended Hoffmann families, perhaps Aunt Elizabeth and Uncle Charlie would take them into their family and take care of them. Ruth also remembered that Aunt Louise was not married and had no way of supporting them so that was not a possibility.

Even as a child, this all must have been a terrible shock to me for I don't remember a thing that happened for some time afterward; our trip to St. Louis for my mother's burial or anything until I was taken to Springfield, Ill. to see the twins in an orphan's home. They had been Christened and named; one Wilhelm and the other Frederick. They only lived about six months. The home was no place for them for they could have had a good home with a very nice couple in Mt. Pulaski if he wanted to adopt them but Uncle Will, their father, wouldn't allow it. He didn't think anyone was good enough to bring up his sons, therefore depriving me of two brothers.

Editor's Notes: About two weeks after Ruth's mother's death, her Uncle Will and Aunt Louise got Ruth and her brothers ready to take a trip to Springfield, IL. Uncle Will had already made arrangements for an orphanage there to take her twin brothers. This was very upsetting to Ruth. She loved her brothers. She told her Uncle Will and Aunt Louise, "I will help take care of them. Aunt Louise has already taught me how to do all the things that they need". But Ruth's plea was for naught; Uncle Will had already made up his mind to put them into the orphanage. Ruth supposed that he thought that he could not continue to be a pastor at a church if he had to take care of a step daughter and twin baby boys.

Ruth felt real pain over leaving her twin brothers at that orphanage. This was the worst of all possibilities. She sometimes verbally expressed her vexation about taking her brothers to an orphanage, "Surely, one of my married aunts and uncles could have taken the three of us into their family and I could have helped take care of them. My brothers would have had better care than they received at the orphanage and may have lived a long life." In Ruth's mind, leaving the twins at the orphanage also deprived her of siblings, twin brothers. This was a continuing lament openly expressed by Ruth throughout her long life.

Those who knew Ruth well could feel her grief when she talked about her twin brothers and having to leave them at the orphanage; this was true even 80 some years after leaving them at the orphanage.

After my mother's passing, Aunt Louise must have come home with us from St. Louis. She stayed with us until we acquired a housekeeper. She was the Roth's Aunt Kate, a very dear little lady. She had a small cottage a short way out of town where I walked with her in the early evening sometimes. We'd pass lovely blooming locust trees on the way in the spring – 1904 – and beds of pretty pansies blooming in her front yard that I loved so much – those walks also I'll never forget.

It wasn't long before Uncle Will was courting Roth's oldest daughter, Amelia. They were married the summer of 1904[11] and were seen at the St. Louis World's Fair by some members of the family.

Though I never saw Margarite again after moving from Mt. Pulaski, Aunt Amelia got us together through correspondence years later. Margarite married a mister Brady with whom she was very much in love. They had one son, Bill. Years later when her husband had passed on, she went to Tampa, Florida to live with her son Bill and his wife, Joyce. Also, there was Bill and Joyce's daughter and grandson Chris, granddaughter and great grandson that she always wrote so lovingly about. Her family and home there in Tampa were a great help and blessing for her for she missed her dear husband so. She was finally put into a convalescent home needing more care and medical attention. When she was not able to write anymore which I missed very much, her dear letters, Bill and Joyce continued her correspondence, keeping me and friends in touch with her and letting us know how she was getting along. Dear Margarite, she has now passed on – April 30, 1983 which indeed was a blessing after her suffering. For the family also, much as they loved her and will miss her.

Bill, through his correspondence, I know to be a fine sincere man. He was, and perhaps still is, connected with the university there where he lives. He even took over the pulpit when their minister was away so his mother wrote. She often mentioned how much he loved his flower garden and fruit trees and took such good care of them. Bill and Joyce were planning to come to Calif. this summer to visit up north in the area of Ft. Ord where Bill was stationed when in the service. If they come south, I hope they'll stop to see me.

Back to Mt. Pulaski for a moment. During the first few months in Pasadena in 1916, I had a nice room in the home of a Mrs. Young – only $6 a month – can you imagine? And only a couple of blocks away from Main Street, now called Colorado Blvd. One day Mrs. Young had a friend from Los Angeles come to visit her. That evening when she left to board her streetcar at the corner, I walked with them so Mrs. Young would not have to walk home alone. In conversation, the friend mentioned having lived in Springfield, Ill. What a nice surprise to me. I told her that while living in Mt. Pulaski, I had been there several times with my uncle to visit good friend, Rev. Shulski and his 3 daughters. One my age, the other two older. It turned out that the friend knew them well, went to school with the two older daughters. What a pleasant surprise. Small world, so we often say.

Editor's Notes: Ruth accompanied Aunt Louise back to St. Louis. She was told she would live with Aunt Elizabeth and Uncle Charlie for a while until the family could decide with whom she was going to live with on a permanent basis. At first, this seemed to be a fortunate turn of events for Ruth. She thought, "If I could be a good helper for Aunt Elizabeth and Uncle Charlie, they would choose to take me into their family on a permanent basis." That is what Ruth wanted to happen. But that is not what actually happened. No matter how hard Ruth tried to please Aunt Elizabeth, her efforts were for naught.

---

10 Her mother's death was a devastating blow to Ruth while trying to understand the meaning of her life at the young age of eight. Imagine, just over three years after her father died, her mother dies.

11 Uncle Will and Aunt Amelia were married about six months after her mother died.

6

Living with My Uncle William's and Aunt Amelia's Family

Hagerstown, MD, a long way from St. Louis, MO – Age 9 to 11
1904 to 1906 – Hagerstown, MD

After their marriage, Uncle Will and his bride, Aunt Amelia, went to live in Hagerstown, MD where he became pastor of the Lutheran Church. I'm sure the family felt, as my *step* stepfather, he was still responsible for me. So, nearing school time in the early fall, after my pleasant summer in St Louis living with Aunt Elizabeth in 1904; my bag was packed for me, also a good lunch. I was taken to the railroad station by my grandmother; the last time I saw her and Uncle Dan. They put me in the care of the conductor and I was on my way to Hagerstown. It took a day and a night.

The train's steam engines burned coal to provide the source of power to pull the train at that time, and perhaps I was afraid to wash on the train. My Aunt said she had never seen anyone so black, so she immediately put me in a soap bath.[12]

Figure 9 – Coal Burning Steam Engine Train In 1905

Editor's Notes: In the morning of the second day after her arrival at Uncle Will's and Aunt Amelia's apartment in Hagerstown, Uncle Will invited Ruth to sit down in their kitchen to tell her what they expected of her. He reminded her that she was nine years old now and able to be a productive member of their household. He expected her to be worthy of the room and board they provided. She was to be up early every morning, clean out the ashes of the wood burning kitchen cook stove and take the ashes out to the garden. She was to bring in the kindling and wood that would be needed for that day's cooking, and light the fire in the kitchen stove. Then Ruth was to go out to the pump, pump the water to fill the large bucket with drinking water, fill the percolator pot and set it on the stove to be heated so that Uncle Will and Aunt Amelia could have a cup of hot coffee when they came out to the kitchen. During the winter season Ruth was to also clean the ashes out of the fireplace, bring in the wood needed for the day and start that fire in it as well.

Furthermore, when Ruth came home from school, she was to assist

Aunt Amelia in the household chores each day and run errands for Uncle Will as needed. Ruth was also to attend public school daily plus Sunday School classes and worship services each Sunday Ruth had a busy day each day of the week.

It just happened that Aunt Amelia was pregnant by the time Ruth arrived at Hagerstown so she was also asked to help take care of their new son, William Hoffman, when he was born. One can begin to observe Ruth's life developing into another 'Cinderella Story'.

One more thing; she was also to make sure that she was always properly dressed each day and was to conduct all of her conversations and activities in a way that was appropriate for a pastor's niece.

I liked Hagerstown. So different from any place where I'd lived aside from St. Louis. It's more of a city. Many streets named after well-known people like Washington, our street, which crosses Potomac two blocks up in the center of town. Looking in the opposite direction were the Blue Ridge Mountains. Antietam was another well-known name of another street.

Figure 10 – 1905 Hagerstown Looking Down Washington St. From Public Square, copied from Wikipedia

Our two-story brick flat with iron railing along our two step Victorian, all brick, even the walks. On one side of our four-block square was Washington, the side street we lived on. It was indeed interesting and very convenient. Our landlady was a Mrs. Hunter. She was a very nice lady – took me out for an ice cream soda one day which did not agree with me – couldn't look at ice cream for a long time after that. However, I liked the people of Hagerstown and soon became acquainted with many.

My uncle published his own church paper and sent me out to get subscriptions. At one house on Potomac when I rang the bell, who should answer the door but my school teacher, Miss Sands. What a surprise! She had a friend with her but still invited me in for tea, a piece of cake and a glass of milk. That was indeed a treat.

Figure 11 – Mansions Along Potomac St., Hagerstown, MD Circa 1910, copied from Wikipedia

Hagerstown had many lovely big homes on Potomac St., almost from center of town out a way, built on higher ground than the street with terraced gardens, etc. See post card my cousin sent to me when driving through there years later.[13]

Names of some of Uncle Will's parishioners that I remember – Ernst, Loehr, Holzapfel, Himmel. The Ernst's had quite a large family and I remember – lived a short distance beyond Potomac St. on a hill and near the Pope Auto Manufacturing business. I spent many a fun night there with the children. The Loehr's lived nearby. The Holzapfel lived up the street from my school, about a block or so away and across from a large college on the hill. The Himmel's lived downtown near the center on Potomac St. They had a saloon and lived in the same building. They were very nice people and close by were good friends. I remember spending quite a bit of time with them and "Oh! The pretzels they had – so good!" Their son, Bill, had a birthday one day before mine – the 29th of March. Always remember him then. Wonder if he is still there.

Still in Hagerstown with the Holzapfel. My lovely granddaughter, Karen Dill, now Mrs. Kevin Upton Wright[14] of Silver Springs, MD, had a friend, Ruth Holzapfel, from a younger generation of the same family and many years later Karen attended Ruth's wedding about two years ago in 1981. I believe when Karen met Ruth's father, she told him about her grandmother having lived in Hagerstown as a child and that I remembered the Holzapfel and much about the city. He became so interested that he wrote me a nice friendly letter relating different things and parts of the city and that his grandfather had been Mayor of Hagerstown at one time. He asked me to write and let him know what I remembered, which I did – answered his letter but no reply. Karen recently told me that she believes he passed on from a heart attack which was very sad to hear. Had hoped to hear from him again.

Editor's Notes: One day while Ruth was living in Hagerstown, her Uncle Will received a telegram to inform him that his mother, Ruth's grandmother, had died. Ruth loved her grandmother. She wanted to go home to St. Louis to grieve this loss and pay her respect for her grandmother. Ruth would also be able to visit with all of her family she had not seen for nearly one year. Surly, Uncle Will would want to be present at his mother's funeral. But Uncle Will decided that neither of them would go; it was too expensive. Ruth was heartbroken.

My Aunt Amelia had her first baby in Hagerstown, a boy, William, named after his father. She sent me to a Dr. Fahrney one day for cough syrup for him. Somehow the name Fahrney stayed with me. I've always been interested in names. Many years later when I had my own family, a dentist in Glendale was recommended for some special work for one of the girls; his name was Fahrney. The doctors were related and came from a well-known family in Chicago, Ill.

It is always interesting and gives one a good feeling to meet people who live and know the area where you have lived and liked so well. My first two summers in Pasadena were spent taking care of two dear little girls, Alyse and Dana Miller from Hagerstown, MD of all places. They were visiting their grandparents on S. Euclid Ave. The well-known McWilliams, parents of their mother, Mrs. Ganz. Her husband, a doctor and father of the girls, had passed on and she now is married to a Mr. Ganz. There was plenty of help in the large home so all I had to do was keep Alyse and Dana busy and happy. I gave them their lessons in the mornings, afternoon naps, then walks, appointments or whatever; even to a dentist in L.A. one day. When time for school, Alyse and Dana were returning to Hagerstown. I was invited to go along with them but much as I would like to have seen Hagerstown and old school friends, I had no desire to leave California. Mrs. Ganz even knew my friend and neighbor Marian Fury who had become a librarian.

One very pleasant surprise, while taking care of Alyse and

Dana, was a trip to Santa Barbara. My first glimpse of the well-known city. We stayed up at the El Encanto Hotel. That was indeed a pleasure. The well-known chef, Julia Childs, on TV, is a cousin of Alyse and Dana. She is the daughter of Mrs. Ganz's brother, John McWilliams and Julia often came over to play with the girls. Happy days. Even though we had a car and chauffer, grandfather McWilliams at the age of 93 often walked to his office up town several blocks away.

In later years when Mrs. Ganz lived in Pasadena, we often met at Red Cross which was always a pleasure.

Figure 12 – Ruth At Her 20 Year Service Award Day At Red Cross

Editor's Notes: Ruth did volunteer work at the American Red Cross in Pasadena, CA for 26 years. The photograph below shows Ruth wearing her 20-year anniversary ribbon and badge. The ribbon and celebration were given in thanks for her continuous participation at the American Red Cross volunteer activities. Ruth always said, "I loved going to Red Cross and participating in the volunteer acuities there. There were always several of us older women present. We became good friends. We always had a good time catching up with what everyone was doing and exchanging ideas."

Back to Hagerstown, this was where my extended family wanted me to be. I made up my mind that I would do my best to serve my Uncle Will and Aunt Amelia and their family.

---

12 There was no air conditioning on the train so the windows were open all through the day and night to get fresh air into the passenger's compartment during those hot Indian summer days.

13 A Wikipedia photograph, of North Potomac Street circa 1910, is shown here in Figure 9 to illustrate Ruth's memories. Her post card was not found.

14 Ruth's granddaughter Karen now goes by the name, Karen Alexander.

7

Serving as Governess of My Cousins

Becoming a live-in governess for my cousins – Age 10 to 12
1906 to 1907 – Rockport, IN

On the road again. How I loved those train rides. We were on our way to a new home in Rockport, Indiana, not far from Louisville where we changed trains. Rockport was built up high along the Ohio River; a very wide town but only one or two names I remember from there; though my school class is very clear. Thought I was pretty smart one day getting a 92 on my class paper – don't remember my remark to the teacher – though she was very nice – took me down a peg or two.

I will always remember one boy eating dry shredded wheat for a recess snack.

One day I was invited to spend the night with a school friend and her family. I was amazed the next morning at the breakfast table; they served steak, potatoes, etc. a regular dinner. The father may have been a hardworking man and needed the nourishment.

On my way to school one morning at age 11 (eleven) the

newsboys were all over yelling out the sad news of the disastrous San Francisco earth quake in 1906. What a shock even to me as a child and indeed a very sad day for many.

Figure 13 – Rockport Steamboat Landing in Early 1900s - Photograph courtesy of the Indiana Historical Society, General Picture Collection

It's strange, but I don't remember any of the parishioners or much about the church in Rockport. Guess it wasn't exciting enough for me. I do remember a Mrs. Rankin who invited me to dinner the evening before we left Rockport and sitting on the back step shelling the peas. She, I believe, was our music teacher at school, a class I enjoyed very much.

Editor's Notes: Uncle Will and Aunt Amelia seemed to enjoy a good loving relationship, unlike what Uncle Will had with Ruth's mother. Aunt Amelia was soon pregnant again and delivered another child

while they were in Rockport, Indiana. It was another boy. They named him Charles. Now Ruth was in charge of taking care of two baby boys. Both Uncle Will and Aunt Amelia showed much care and love for each of their two boys. But this love was not extended to Ruth.

One of the daily chores still vivid in Ruth's mind was having to help Aunt Amelia wash the dirty diapers each day. There were no washing machines or electric dryers in the early 1900s so she had to help wash the diapers by hand, hang them up to dry on an outdoor clothesline and then gather and fold them each day so that they had enough diapers for the two boys for the next day. This chore had to be done daily. It was in addition to her other regular daily chores. Even though this chore was not pleasant for Ruth, she wanted to please her Uncle Will and Aunt Amelia so Ruth did this chore without ever complaining.

8

Learning How Others Worked Through Their Troubles

Going to a new parish in Pennsylvania – Age 12 to 13
1907 to 1908 – South Fork, PA

Our next move was to South Fork, PA, a coal mining town. A lot of Hungarians there, coal miners. Neighbors across from our church and parsonage were miners. That was the first time I had seen a black person married to a white; the man black, the woman white. Other members of the family, white and very nice neighbors. On the corner of our block lived a sweet old colored woman who often sat outside smoking her pipe. We called her "Smokins".

A big new school building was being built while we were in South Fork. So, my school days there were very few that year. My uncle also had another church some miles out into the country. We took the train in South Fork to go there. On the way to that church, we passed the remains of the dam which burst, releasing the water from the South Fork Reservoir through Johnstown in 1889.

Editor's Notes: Johnstown, PA has experienced many major floods, one each in the years 1889, 1907, 1936 and 1977, each causing the death of many and extensive damage to the town. The "Great Flood" of May 31, 1889 caused at least 2,209 people's death as a result of that flood and subsequent fire that raged through the debris. The aftermath of the flood that occurred in 1889 is the one whose devastation Ruth Hoffmann saw firsthand and heard the local folk recall the devastation remaining in their memories.

The railroad station was close to a bridge under which flowed the Conemaugh River. The railroad station was built up on higher ground along the tracks that had a few steps leading down to the main street which was almost completely covered with water on one of my trips there; had to take the next train home.

Figure 14 – Johnstown City Hall Showing Flood Height Markers, copied from Wikipedia

After the big flood, people who could afford it, built their homes on the hills overlooking the city. One family, the Thomas' that I met some years later in California, owned the big department store in Johnstown and built their home on the hill. I had visited their department store in Johnstown, PA when I lived in South Fork. More about the Thomas' later. The Foxes of South Fork were friends of theirs. They lived across from the Johnstown Post Office. I knew their home well.[16]

Back[17] to the country church in South Fork. The only name I remember there is Miller, their daughter's name, Thelma, with whom I played. We were with the Miller's quite often. Johnstown was quite a few miles from South Fork so going there was by train. My Uncle sent me there on errands and subscriptions to his church paper. On one trip I lost my return ticket so started walking home along the tracks. I knew that I would not make it alone and in the dark so I stopped at the signal tower. The man there was very understanding and signaled the 8 o'clock train to stop and I was on my way home. Fortunately, a Miss or Mrs. Short, a school teacher, who lived near us was on the train so we came home together.

Editor's Notes: Aunt Amelia became pregnant again and delivered their third child while they were in South Fork, Pennsylvania. It was their third boy and they named him, Harold. Now Ruth was in charge of taking care of three boys, two in diapers, each about one year older than the next. Perhaps the most difficult responsibility and challenge for Ruth was to find the right activities to keep the boys interested and happy so that they did not make so much noise that would interrupt Uncle Will's study and preparation for his Sunday sermon

---

16 *Ruth often mentioned the Johnstown flood and personally seeing the devastation and flood markers on the Johnstown City Hall (see Figure 14).*

17 This paragraph was originally positioned after the next paragraph but since it is a continuation of her memories in South Fork, it is brought forward.

9

Moving on to Gallitzin, PA

A short train ride to our new parish – Age 13 to 14
1908 to 1909 – Gallitzin, PA

My uncle's next church was in Gallitzin, PA, a little farther East. He also had a church in another town near Bessemer [18]. Gallitzin had many railroads – a width of them and the town built up on both sides with a high bridge built up over the tracks for vehicles and safer walking. One could cross the tracks also and I suppose it was closer to home for many. The Post Office was right across from the tracks from the station, where "The Philly", they called it, dropped off the mail every evening about 8 o'clock. The mail was distributed immediately with many people (*physically present*) for theirs. I was usually there to pick up my uncle's mail.

A good-looking church was built in Gallitzin while my uncle was pastor there and I think he was well liked. A group of young people there adored him and they often got together for meetings, etc. We were often invited to parishioner's homes for dinner and we never saw a busier group than the Ladies Aiders as we called them, holding quilting gatherings, church suppers, etc. We lived in a home apart from the church. Often wonder why we didn't stay there longer.

Altoona was some miles east of Gallitzin. I was sent there on an errand one day by train. The trip took us around the well-known "Horse Shoe Bend" both coming and going. It was so exciting seeing the whole train going around this curve.

Editor's Note: Ruth is referring to the well-known Horse Shoe Curve on the rail line going over the Appalachian Mountains between Altoona and Johnstown, Pennsylvania. As a passenger on a train, one can look out the window and see both the engine and the last car of the train. This rail line was constructed by manual labor using only picks, shovels and axes in mid-19th century, well before Caterpillar tractors, bulldozers and back hoes were invented, and the first trains traveled around this curve in 1854. The train tracks reach an altitude of 1,572 feet above sea level at this Land Mark. From the tourist sight, one has a 220-degree view; the diameter across the two sides of the curve is about 1,000 feet and one can see about 2,375 feet of track. At this sight the trains climb/drop about nine feet for every mile traveled. This site is now designated as a National Historic Civil Engineering Landmark.

The only thing I remember about the other small town near Gallitzin is one night when we stayed overnight with members of Uncle Will's church. Wild berries were very plentiful and the picking fun. I loved the Allegheny Mountains.

Editor's Notes: Ruth told us, "Aunt Amelia became pregnant again and delivered their fourth child while we were in Gallitzin, Pennsylvania. This time it was a girl. They named her Dorothy. Now I was in charge of taking care of three boys and a baby girl, each about one year older than the next. Helping to take care of four young children was certainly a challenge and the source of much stress for me to find the right activities to keep three young boys and a baby girl entertained so that they did not make so much noise that would interrupt Uncle Will's study and preparation for his Sunday's sermon. And all the while, I had to continue my school work and do all of my daily chores."

All through the Spring and Summer of 1909, Ruth was feeling a low-level pain in her jaw. Soon after school started, the pain level grew worse. Both Aunt Amelia and Uncle Will looked to see if there were any cavities but they could not see anything that was wrong. There was no dentist in Gallitzin and it was too far to go to Johnstown. Ruth just had to bear the pain. There was also the problem of not having enough money to pay for a dentist to fix the cause of the pain. Ruth had to grin and bear this continuing pain.

---

18 Ruth remembered the wrong town name for the second church. This is the name of the town in upper Michigan where her Uncle Will was assigned before her mother died. There is a Bessemer, PA but it is hundreds of miles distant from Gallitzin.

10

Living in Silver Lake Indiana

Taking the train to a New Church in Indiana – Age 14 to 15
1909 to 1910 – Silver Lakes, IN

One more jaunt with my aunt and uncle and family; on the way to Silver Lake, Indiana. Four children in the family by now, Bill, Charles, Harold, and Dorothy. Wish I still had the picture of them taken there. Dorothy in the wagon, Bill supposedly pulling it and Charles and Harold standing with them. Indiana was quite different from Pennsylvania – flat ground, many farms and very nice people.

The Leonard's, church members, are the only ones I remember – were always so good to us. I remember spending many a happy hour with them. They had 2 lovely grown daughters. There was a fun group of girls there my age, 14. The only one whose name I remember was Lucy Underhill. The latter one, the name of the street I now live on at 88 years of age, Underhill Terrace in California. I often played with a doctor's daughter; she was a cripple. Years later I met her aunt at a party in Los Angeles and she couldn't believe that I knew her niece in Silver Lake. It was a busy town with farmers in and out. Revival meetings in tents and there was a band stand on one corner in the center of town with several steps up to where the musicians sat. One Halloween, boys hoisted a cow up there; wonder how they ever got it down.

Silver Lake was a very pleasant mid-western town with only the necessary businesses for one that size and a very good residential section. Many nice-looking two-story houses. We also had one with a fairly large vegetable garden. I know for I did my share of hoeing and watering. Our home had no bathroom or helpful facilities to make life a bit easier as we have it today. Baths were taken in a large galvanized tub in what may have been called the summer kitchen then with plain board flooring. Aunt Amelia did her best and I'm sure was a real good homemaker. It wasn't an easy life that's for sure. Always remember her making a big pan of popcorn on Sunday afternoons which was a good treat.

Our Church, only a block away, was practically downtown. The one and only school nearby.

My uncle also had a church in the country some distance from Silver Lake. He had to hire a horse and buggy from the livery stable to get out there. I often went with him. After church we were always invited to dinner at the home of one of the parishioners. And what delicious dinners they were. I'll never forget. There was always chicken, homemade breads and pie.

Our whole family was invited to one of the threshing sessions on one of the farms. The farmers got together and helped each other with their threshing – quicker and easier that way I suppose. And while the men were out working, the wives were busy in the kitchen cooking a delicious dinner for the threshers and all.

My one day alone, invited to the farm of Mr. and Mrs. Giffle was a fun day for me – feeding the chickens, gathering eggs and there were many. Also watching Mrs. Giffle preparing pie for the oven. There were other things we did I'm sure but do not remember. Anyway, a different and happy day for me.[19]

However, I was soon to leave my home with Uncle Will and family. I had been suffering with neuralgia on the right side of my face due to lack of dental work. A dentist nearby, his daughter Catherine and I good friends, evidently was not able to do the required work on them. Calcium, I was told later, is what I lacked so to get the proper care, I left Silver Lake for St. Louis at age 15.[20]

Editor's Notes: During Ruth's stay in Silver Lake, Aunt Amelia did not become pregnant again. Although she never thought about it at the time, Ruth noted that serving as a nanny for these four children was helping her to become a well-practiced nanny and children's governess in Ruth's future life.

For the past year, Ruth was having an increasing pain in her jaw. The dentist in Silver Lake did not know how to treat the pain and it was too far to go to Indianapolis where there would be a dentist who could treat her. There was also the fear of not having enough money to pay for a dentist to fix the problem. Perhaps, God, through His providence had a way to facilitate Ruth's going back to St. Louis without causing a problem with Uncle Will and Ruth's extended family.

One morning Uncle Will announced that Ruth would be going back to St. Louis. Ruth was jubilant. Her prayers were answered After Ruth's health and dental problems became so painful, the Hoffmann family finally decided to send her back to St. Louis so that Uncle Charlie could give her a physical examination, Ruth could get her teeth fixed and she would have some time to restore her good health. On that long all-day train ride to St. Louis, Ruth again seriously hoped, imagined and prayed that one of her extended Hoffmann families would take her in and love her as one of their own family.

19 It is worthy to note how much Ruth enjoyed her "one day alone" mentioned above. Her daily chores and daily care of her four cousins were never ending.

20 Ruth's trip back to St. Louis, MO probably took place about mid-April, 1910, perhaps soon after Ruth's 15th birthday. We know that Ruth is not listed in the US Federal Census of Kosciusko County, IN, which was taken on 18 April, 1910. We also know that Ruth does appear in the St. Louis County Supplementary Sheet of the US Census of St. Louis County, MO, that was taken on 28 April, 1910. There is but a ten day gap between the posting date of these two censuses so Ruth's travels from Silver Lake, Indiana to St. Louis took place between 1 April to 25 April, 1910.

11

Returning Home to St. Louis

Going back to St. Louis, MO to Recuperate – Age 15
1910 – St. Louis, MO

Uncle Will took me to the railroad station. I don't remember leaving or boarding a train. But, once on the way, I'll never forget the many beautiful, attractive farms we passed on the way to Indianapolis. May have changed trains there to go on to St. Louis.

Think that was the trip when cousin Walter met me at the station in St. Louis. He in his early twenties must have been way embarrassed when my string of beads broke scattering them all over the place.

I stayed at Aunt Elizabeth's home while my dental work was being done. Uncle Charlie sent me to a good dentist he knew where I spent many hours. Finally finished, I had four good looking upper front pivot teeth. To make them appear more my own at that age, the dentist added one bit of gold to one of the teeth and they looked very good for a long time.

Editor's Note: All through the time Ruth was having her teeth fixed, she continued to hope and pray that one of the Hoffmann families would take her in to live with them. It did not turn out that way though. Instead, when her dental work was completed, Ruth was told that she was to live with a young couple named Guy and Lizzie Smith. Ruth did not know them. This was a very sad day for Ruth; her hopes were shattered again. She was not going to be taken in by one of her several Hoffmann families that lived in St. Louis. On the other hand, she thought, "Thank heavens, I will not have to go back to live with Uncle Will and Aunt Amelia." Not wanting to be a problem for her extended Hoffmann family, Ruth did move her things into the apartment in which Guy and Lizzie Smith were living, just as she was told to do.

Based on genealogical research performed, it is believed that Guy and Lizzie Smith are not of any relation to Ruth even though she is listed in the 1910, Supplemental Sheet of the St. Louis, MO census as their niece. This census was taken on 28 April of that year soon after all of Ruth's dental work was completed.

All of the personal information listed for this Ruth Hoffmann is appropriate for our Ruth except it says Ruth is Guy and Lizzie Smith's niece. Ruth did not mention Guy and Lizzie Smith in her Memoirs and she never mentioned having lived with an Uncle Guy and Aunt Lizzie Smith to the Editor in any of the many stories she told of her life. Also, no relatives with these names were found in the genealogic research made for the Julius and Sophia Hoffmann family. This short interval of Ruth's life remains a mystery.

12

Learning a Marketable Trade

Living with the Gerdes Sisters, Learning How to Sew – Age 15
1910 – St. Louis, MO

My next step was to get a job and earn my own living but then something wonderful happened. Two maiden ladies, Freda and Lillie Gerdes, who lived next door to Aunt Elizabeth, became interested in me and asked me to come and live with them. Their invitation was readily accepted. I liked them so much and they were so good to me. They became Aunt Lillie and Aunt Freda to me.[21] Aunt Lillie kept house and Aunt Freda, a model, had her own dress making business right in the home. The front part of the basement done over and equipped for that purpose.

Editor's Notes: Having lived next door to Ruth's Aunt Elizabeth and Uncle Charlie for most of their lives, Freda and Lillie Gerdes and their brother Herman got to know Ruth well during Ruth's many visits with Aunt Elizabeth and Uncle Charlie over the past 15 years. and Ruth knew the Gerdes sisters very well. Freda and Lillie were present at the funeral services held for each of Ruth's parents, grandparents and twin brothers. They also knew of Ruth's desire to be part of one of the local Hoffmann families rather than live afar from St. Louis with her Uncle William and Aunt Amelia for the past six years.

The Gerdes sisters felt great empathy for Ruth's situation. Upon seeing that Ruth was not taken in by one of the St. Louis Hoffmann families, the Gerdes sisters decided to invite Ruth to live with them. She would be living local within St. Louis. Ruth could help them by learning the sewing and dress making business. You can hear the joy in Ruth's words contained in this chapter of her life. The Gerdes sister's invitation was welcomed and appreciated. Ruth's prayers were answered. She was once again looking forward towards a good future.

There was also a bachelor brother there, Uncle Herman. A very nice quiet man who loved his music. He had a good Victor Victrola on which he played his red sealed records, opera and the best of everything.[22] We had music all day on Sundays excepting the time he spent at his work bench in the shed.

Figure 15 – 1910 Victor Victrola Acoustical Record Player

Being in the dress making business, Aunt Freda and Aunt Lillie were always well dressed. So was I, thanks to Aunt Freda. She catered to the elite and designed many a beautiful gown. The satins and materials so beautiful then and she always got first choice of them from the good shop especially from Schrage, Vanderwood and Barney where she was well known.

Several very nice women were employed by her and the sewing machines at the time, the Wilcox and Gibbs chainstitch, did very fine stitching. The women were good workers and congenial. Aunt Freda always served them coffee in the mornings and afternoon, usually with cake or a good nibble of some kind. Both sisters were kind, generous, and helpful to everyone and they were rewarded in return. For one, "believe-it-or-not", their grocer came to their home every Saturday morning to pick up their grocery order and delivered it later.

Aunt Lillie was a fine cook and baker. I'll never forget her good rolls and coffee cakes. She and I were left quite busy with the house, always kept in good order. Aunt Freda, being somewhat of an artist, kept the house looking very attractive, always the latest in curtains, wall décor, etc. The house a two-story brick flat with large basement windows even with the ground outside, giving light to the workroom in the basement. There were good tenants upstairs, the Straubs. They used the main front entrance, stairway in the hall. One baby girl in the family. Mrs. Straub did beautiful China paintings – plates mostly.

We lived well, everything the best; loved the opera and good shows. Often played cards Saturday evening with friends who lived near O'Fallon Park or they came to our house. Many a sweet Sunday afternoon was spent visiting a park or some well-known garden where we enjoyed the flowers. Aunt Freda was an expert gardener. In fact, I don't think there was anything she couldn't do.

She always kept the yard looking so pretty in the summertime with pretty flowers and a beautiful vine, I think called a night blooming cereus. It grew up on a trellis on the side of the porch and the flower at night looked like large white lilies.[23] The three of us sitting in the swing enjoying our nice big bowl of fruit-Jell-O which we did quite often.

One place where we liked to go on picnics was to the Chain of Rocks Park, quite some distance from home but transportation as usual, the streetcar. Uncle Herman often rode his tandem taking one of his nurses along. Overlooking the land from the park which was on rather high ground, it looked just like the farms in Indiana. Chain of Rocks Park was the location of the Municipal Waterworks System, a perfect spot for an outing.

In time, I had friends of my own, Miss Minnie, Aunt Freda's right-hand worker had nieces and nephews nearby who became good friends. Next door to them a church I attended for a while and sang in the choir. Ruth Stumpi, Uncle Charlie's niece, his sister's daughter, also a good friend I'd known since quite young and with dozens to visit and Aunt Elizabeth right next door, I never lacked for some place to go. Almira, still my big sister, often surprised me with some goodies even at that age. Occasionally went to church with Aunt Elizabeth and Uncle Charlie. Most of all though, I enjoyed the service on Sunday at the Christian Science Church out on Lindell Blvd.

There was a third Gerdes sister, a Mrs. Koenitzer, who lived in Saginaw, Mich. She came to visit her sisters while I was there. We became good friends and one day she took me out to lunch alone to get better acquainted I presumed. I enjoyed being with her. She was quite a jolly person but I never dreamed then that I'd be living with her and Mr. Koenitzer in another year.

---

21 Because of their mutual love, Ruth affectionately honors the Gerdes family.

22 Enrico Caruso (1873-1921) was an Italian tenor who was the foremost Metropolitan

Opera attraction and an early recording artist. These old recordings were played on acoustic players with large sound horns. There were no electronic record players at that time.
23 Four o'clock flower (Mirabilis Jalapa) blossom usually opens with a pop only in the late afternoon at dusk.

13

Living With Mother and Father Koenitzer

Living with Mother and Father Koenitzer – Age 16 to 21
1911 to 1916 – Saginaw, MI

The time arrived and I was very sad at leaving Aunt Lillie and Aunt Freda when they had been so good to me but everything seemingly had been arranged and agreeable with all so, off I went to Saginaw. And indeed, another step up for me. The flat in St. Louis where the Gerdes' lived belonged to the Koenitzers and is where they lived before Saginaw.

Mr. and Mrs. Koenitzer were like a father and mother to me. I was practically adopted. Mother K. even had calling cards printed for me with my name "Ruth Koenitzer" on them. Very much the fashion at that time to leave your card when calling on friends, especially new ones. Still have one. Teas, luncheons and card parties were popular in Saginaw, very social.

Editor's Notes: Mr. Robert Koenitzer and Johanne Gerdes Koenitzer gave their love to Ruth Hoffmann and demonstrated that love by taking her in to live with them as their daughter. They included her in all of the family and social activities in which they were involved. Mother Koenitzer taught Ruth all of the social graces appropriate for a young lady born in that era. For the next five years, Ruth assumed the surname of Koenitzer and lived with "Mother and Father Koenitzer" in Saginaw, MI. Even the name Ruth Koenitzer appears in the 1914 Saginaw City Registry. These are good years for Ruth. Their most important gift to Ruth was she is feeling loved again.

This informal adaption was good for the Koenitzers as well. Ruth gave them her love and respect as well as being their lovely and gracious "daughter" in all of their personal and social activities. The Koenitzers had only one child, a daughter, Ella, who had earlier visited Germany, met and in time married a German citizen and they established their home in Germany. Still desiring to have a daughter to love and share their home, Robert and Johanne Koenitzer reached out to Ruth and took her in as their informally adapted daughter.

Since Ruth was still not of an emancipating age, it is assumed that the several extended Hoffmann families agreed to this arrangement for Ruth never mentions any objection by them. The Hoffmann families all knew where Ruth was living since the Koenitzers had once lived next door to Ruth's Aunt Elizabeth and Uncle Charlie Millies and all of the Hoffmann families knew the Koenitzers well.

There was a strong mutual love between Ruth and Mother Koenitzer, a true mother/daughter bond. This was the mutual love bond that Ruth had desired and missed since her mother's death. One can feel this mother/daughter love in her writings contained herein.

Looking back at Ruth's six years of service to her Aunt Amelia and Uncle Will from another point of view, Johanne Koenitzer was also fulfilling the literal role of "Fairy God Mother" in Ruth's own "Cinderella Story". Ruth was finally relieved of her daily chores she had to do for her Aunt Amelia and Uncle Will for the past six years. She was now living in a large home with servants, the home was situated in a lovely resort community in Saginaw, MI, and Ruth was learning the finer points of an affluent social life. Ruth had become a beautiful young lady. She sometimes served as host of teas, luncheons and card parties for the Koenitzer family and their friends. She was also invited to and attend parties and luncheons hosted by other affluent families.

Ruth was meeting and getting to know many new families, some of whom had eligible bachelors of marrying age. Sometimes Ruth would dream of one of these eligible young men as being her 'Prince Charming' who would ask her to dance; they would fall in love, get married and live happily ever after. After telling this part of the story, Ruth would jokingly add, "I can dream, can't I?"

Figure 16 – Ruth At 16 Years Of Age In Saginaw, MI

Mother K told me later that she had seen me as a baby at Aunt

Elizabeth's. However, the reason for their moving, Father K had a fine, big tannery business in St. Louis. His name was even in some of the school books as inventor of some of the machinery. They, very well off at that time, but he unknowingly made some very poor investments and just about lost everything. Then the move to Saginaw where their friends, the Archers who had a summer home next to theirs at Pointe Aux Braque's, Michigan, a beautiful resort along Lake Heron. In Saginaw, Mr. K went back into the tannery business and all was well. In the office a couple of fine young men, some of good friends from St. Louis helping along with the business and everything seemingly on top of the world again.

Our home, a three story one with a well-furnished basement, one corner the kitchen and breakfast room with a dumb-waiter to upstairs to the main dining room. There was also a washroom and furnace room closed off with doors and best of all a nice cold cellar room where Mother K kept her goodies tucked away. There was usually a good cake ready for serving and wine.

Father Koenitzer made his own wine using wonderful grapes, usually had two barrels in the making. Upstairs, main floor, there was a fireplace with a big mirror above, the hallway big as a room, an attractive stairway going up with railing open to the front.

The big front porch a very pleasant place to sit, swing, do some knitting or reading on summer afternoons which we enjoyed quite often. Good neighbors were always welcome to stop in for a chat and a cup of coffee.

Next door lived the Utters, mother and daughter, a school teacher – next door to them, the Kampforts, always busy planning a card party; Five Hundred, the going game at the time. Later bridge. I suppose daughter Dorothy and I good friends (see picture on our front porch. (*Photograph was not found.*)

Figure 17 – Ruth In Saginaw, MI Circa 1915

Across the street our good friends and neighbors the Fordneys. Mr. Joseph W. Fordney was a well-known congressman for years. His name in our encyclopedia in connection with the Fordney-McCumbers Tariff Act of 1922. The Fordneys were the most generous and caring people, always sharing what they had with friends and neighbors. They had a lovely big home surrounded by a large garden area, even had their own cow, all taken care of by two gardeners. Also, our place which was owned by one of the daughters. They, like Mr. Koenitzer, also made their own wine.

There were only four daughters left at home, this in about 1918, Theodora, Mary and Grace twins and my age, and Agnes an older daughter out of a family of eleven children. The others were married and away from home. Agnes married later while she was still in Saginaw and we were invited to a lovely party afterwards in their home across the way. Chester, the youngest son married the daughter of his commanding officer in the Marines (see clippings. Clippings were not found.)

When son Joe was home on vacation from Aberdeen, Wash. where he helped manage their lumber camps, he'd come over quite often evenings to play cards with us. He was handsome, lots of fun and a very likable fellow. The Fordneys were Catholic, the younger girls attended parochial school at home and then Georgetown Convent in Washington, DC. They were often able to attend congressional sessions with their dad, telling me all about it when they returned home.

Point Aux Braque's was on Flat-Rock Point, (Grindstone City), Saginaw Bay on one side, Lake Huron on the other side. It was a lovely summer resort, occupied mostly by St. Louisans and people from Detroit. Our trip there was by train, changing at Bad Axe. It was always a pleasure and fun to be there. Nothing to do but sleep and eat, take long walks in the woods and when nothing else to do, play cards. On one trip we had the pleasure of a ride on one of the Coast Guard boats.

On a walk to the railroad station, one day we saw Mr. Firestone Sr. of Firestone Tire Co. His family had three or so cottages there. The son, small then and nurses all over the place.

I don't ever remember Clara Orchard being in her cottage next door when we were up there but I enjoyed many visits and meals in her home in Saginaw. She and Mother K best friends, both with a bit of gardener in them. Clara grew the best asparagus, always cut underground and cooked and eaten white instead of green as most people buy it today. She had fine gooseberry bushes also.

Gooseberries make the best pie.

Mother K *(more precisely her gardener)* grew a variety of vegetables, kale, I remember most of all. It had to be frosted before being used. She also had a few chickens which she kept in the washroom during the winter months – well housed and sheltered, providing us with eggs as usual. Every Saturday morning Mother K prepared and made the best raised doughnuts with a spoonful of jam in the center. "Featherbeds", we called them. She always took a bowl full over to the Fordneys for their breakfast.

Mother and Father K. had one daughter, Ella. She had gone to school in Germany, met and later married a Mr. Spaltholz over there and now with three lovely children lived, in Dresden. Spaltholz, in English, means split wood. For any big social occasion, they always had their ice cream made into the shape of a log with a hatchet stuck in the top as if to split wood. Unusual, yes?

Anyway, Mother K was planning on a trip later to visit Ella and family. In the meantime, the war not over as yet[24], she and I spent many a happy hour in her sewing room making clothes for her grandchildren – evidently hard to get at that time. They were sent a roundabout way and fortunately always received. Sometime later, Mother K made the trip to Germany to visit her family. Know how happy they must have been to see her. While she was gone, I kept house and learned enough about the cooking and their way of eating to carry on – even to serving luncheon to Father K and a business friend or two.

Summertime, during a quiet time in Aunt Freda's business, she came to Saginaw to stay with us for a while. She was good company and very helpful with everything.

Minnie Koerner, wife of one of their good friend's son from St. Louis, and in the business with Father K, was indeed a good friend. I spent quite a bit of time with her while Mother K was gone. She was so helpful in many ways. She had a dear baby boy who gave us a lot of pleasure. Minnie became a marvelous cook and did a great deal of entertaining. She was even mentioned in the "Time Cook Book" (clipping in the Time envelope) – (clipping not found).

Editor's Notes: During the time Mother K. was visiting her daughter in Germany, Ruth had much time alone to review her situation and time to reflect on the outcome of several potential paths she could take into her future life. She knew that this was going to be a turning point in her life; she wanted to make the right choice so she could be productive and happy throughout the rest of her life.

First, Ruth personally acknowledged that she was no longer a child. She was now an adult but was depending on the Koenitzers for her living. She was nearly 21 years old and had no eligible man affectionately pursuing her for marriage. Moreover, being 20 years old, she had a diminishing chance of finding a suitable partner for marriage; many of her family and friends were now considering her as becoming an "Old Maid".

*Perhaps the feelings Ruth experienced were the Holy Spirit urging her to take charge of her life. Inwardly, she knew it was time to make the decision to earn her own way in life; able to become meaningfully employed and living a good life among her friends and family. This was one of her most important life decisions. It took a lot of courage for Ruth to see who she was and choose a new, interesting life for herself, a life that was **not** chosen for her by someone else in the Hoffmann family.*

Second, Ruth recognized that it was unlikely that she would be married in the near future for she had no eligible bachelors currently pursuing her with whom she would like to live the rest of her life. If she was going to remain single throughout her life, she needed to possess an occupational skill that would enable her to not only earn a decent living but also enable her to accumulate a sizeable savings through the future years on which she could live on during her old age.[25]

Having spent many years being the caretaker and governess for her Uncle Will's and Aunt Amelia's children, she knew that she could always be a good children's governess. But as a governess, she would still be living with and under the rule of another family.

Ruth had also learned some things about sewing and being a seamstress when she was living with Aunt Freda and Aunt Lillie in St. Louis and observed that Aunt Freda was able to support herself as well as her brother and sister as a dress designer and seamstress. But to become as capable as Freda, Ruth knew that she must first serve as an apprentice during which time she must not only learn the skills of a good seamstress and dress designer well but she would also need to learn the financial part of this business.

Thoughtfully, Ruth made the decision to acquire the occupational skills of a seamstress and dress designer and establish her own sewing business. The best place for her to learn and practice these skills was to become an apprentice of Freda Gerdes. The next morning after she made this important decision, Ruth announced it to Mother and Father Koenitzer at breakfast. Though it was a surprise to them, they both happily agreed that this was the right time for her to go back to St. Louis, work as an apprentice to Aunt Freda to become an excellent seamstress and also learn how to cater to her clients and financially run her own thriving business just as Aunt Freda was doing it.

It was painful for Ruth to think about leaving Mother and Father Koenitzer. For five years they had served well as her adopted parents. Ruth savored the mother/daughter bond that she and Mother Koenitzer had. But she knew she had to do this if she was ever going to be able to live a good and fulfilled life. She had to pack her things, say goodbye to all of her friends there in Saginaw, make arrangements for her travel by railroad to St. Louis, and reserve a room at the YMCA for her first night in St. Louis. It was Ruth's plan to make her coming back to St. Louis a *surprise to all of her friends and family there.*

In the six years previous to her living in Saginaw, Ruth had learned to do good hard daily work while she lived with her Uncle Will and Aunt Amelia. She had learned the value of a good work ethic and would always do her chores even when she did not feel well. But, above all the duties, Ruth was always eager to pitch in to help do whatever needed to be done. She was an accomplished worker for she had learned to do most of the usual daily-life chores well for her uncle and aunt by doing them over and over for six years.

On the other hand, living with the Koenitzers for these past five years, Ruth had also learned the more refined manners and skills needed to socialize and entertain those who were more affluent. These nearly five years living with the Koenitzers in Saginaw were like a finishing school for Ruth. She was now a knowledgeable, well-rounded, single young woman.

Ruth was indeed a beautiful eligible young lady. She was also physically and mentally ready to meet her one true love who would sweep her off her feet, have a beautiful wedding and go off to birth and raise their own family.

---

24 Ruth is referring to World War I, "The War to End All Wars."

25 There was no Social Security safety net for the elderly at this time. The Social Security Act was signed by President Roosevelt on 14 August, 1935, twenty some years after this courageous decision was made by Ruth.

14

Learning the Sewing Business

Becoming Able to Live on My Own – Age 20
1915 – St Louis, MO

It wasn't too long after Mother K returned from Germany that I had the feeling of wanting to be more independent. Also, though all was going well, I had the feeling that I was one too many in the home for Father K. Whether he was not well, I'll not know what it was but I was soon on my way back to St. Louis and the Gerdes's home.

Mrs. Fordney and Mother K. took me to the railroad station. The day before I left Saginaw, Mr. Fordney rode downtown on the street car with me. It was only a few blocks and the last thing he said to me was, "If you ever want to come back, Ruth, and the folks across the way are gone, you come stay with us,"

It was a sad time for me. I hated to leave Mother K; she had been so good to me but it seemed for the best. We had been real pals. I never knew any one quite like her. No matter what happened, she could see the bright side and always make one feel better.

On my way to St. Louis again. Arrangements had been made for a room for me at the YWCA in St. Louis. I arrived and spent my first night there, calling Aunt Freda in the morning to let them know where I was. She was really shocked and came downtown immediately to take me home.

There I stayed for the next few months. Most of my time was spent in the workroom learning all I could about the sewing business to enable me to get a job. Both aunts so kind and helpful. I in turn making myself useful about the home. Some of my time was spent next door at Aunt Elizabeth's and other relatives. It was good to be back in St. Louis.

Thought as long as I have a picture (in envelope- picture not found) and still with Aunt Freda, I'd mention the fun boat trip earlier that she had arranged for all of us, always inviting friends, also cousin Almira on one trip. The boat rides up the Mississippi were a great pleasure, finally reaching the locks, going through them and then on up the Illinois River to Kampsville where she had made reservations for our stay overnight. It was very woodsy there and just fun being out in the open. Aunt Freda, always interested in plants, was bringing home ferns that she had dug up in the woods. On the one trip, it being Sunday, we attended the Catholic Church.

Also, earlier I failed to mention two of Gerdes nieces, Hanna and Martha, daughters of a deceased brother. Lovely girls and good friends but busy with school and their own interests; so, we didn't see them too often. Hanna married later moving to California and Martha who had become a high school teacher married the principal, David H. Weir, who lived to be 90.

Editor's Notes: Ruth worked many hours per day with Aunt Freda and paid attention to her many hints and directions. She had not only learned how to sew well, but she had also learned to make the proper stiches in a smooth, even cadence that all excellent seamstresses did. She learned how to measure a woman's body in preparation for designing and making a new dress, coat and undergarments specifically for that customer.

She could not only design and make these clothing items, she could also make good estimates for the amount of material and labor needed to complete each custom outfit. She also learned Aunt Freda's way of accounting for the cost of material; time spent to cut, sew and make fittings of a new outfit; plus, what percentage she should add for her profit for doing each new job. As the months passed, Ruth felt more and more certain that she could get a job as a seamstress at most tailoring stores anywhere in St. Louis. Even though she was busy working all day long, Ruth was happy with her decision. She added, "I knew this was the right thing for me to be doing."

In good time, Ruth not only felt confident that she could get a job as a seamstress at most tailoring stores anywhere but she also became convinced she could also operate her own dress designing and seamstress shop. She then began to seriously ponder where she should establish her own sewing business; should it be there in St. Louis close to her family roots or in some other distant city. It soon became clear to Ruth that she would have to make a another very important and courageous life decision.

Hearing about Ruth's return to St. Louis and being an apprentice to learn the sewing business, Ruth's Aunt Mary Bleibtreu who lived in Ocean Park, California invited her to come to California to begin her new business. That was certainly a new thought; an interesting but scary thought, so far away from her family and friends. Ruth had only read about California; it was so far away, but they did not have snow in the winter time. It sounded like a good place to live. To seriously consider such big and important move meant Ruth would need to go to the library to read about life in California in the encyclopedia and think long and hard about it. She could not just call Aunt Mary on the telephone for "out of area" calls were not available in these early years of telephone service.

Gradually through these additional nine months of apprenticeship to Aunt Freda, Ruth became sure that she now possessed the skills of a full-fledged seamstress and dress designer. Moreover, if she opened her own business, she could make a very good life for herself using these newly learned skills. Through her research at the library, she became intrigued by the life she imagined she would live if she began her new life in California. Even there, Ruth felt secure that she would have Aunt Mary and Uncle George plus several of her cousins close by – she would not be all alone. And who knows, perhaps her one true love might be waiting for her there. In the next few weeks, she made her second important decision: Ruth would travel to Los Angeles, California to begin her new life as a seamstress there.

Ruth first informed Aunt Freda and Aunt Lillie about her decision. About one week later, at Aunt Elizabeth's Sunday brunch, Ruth told her Hoffmann family about her big decision. At first there were many questions about the wisdom of her decision, "She would be all alone without family!". In time the conversations slowly settled down to congratulations and wishes of well-being from all of her friends and family in her new life in California.

"The cat was now out of the bag!" Ruth was going to live in California. She had to set a date to leave, make arrangements with Aunt Mary in California to have someone to meet her at the Los Angeles train station, and say goodbye to all of her friends and family there in St. Louis. Deep down, Ruth knew that this was not going to be just a visit with family in California and then return. She would probably never be coming back to St. Louis, ever. This would be the last time she would be seeing most of these St. Louis family and friends. This was going to be a major change in Ruth's life.

The Aunts, Lillie and Freda, gave me a lovely going away party before I left; inviting friends and a few relatives. A lovely thoughtful thing to do and nice to see everyone before leaving. Again, it was going to be difficult to leave those who had been so good to me, Aunt Lillie and Aunt Freda and Uncle Herman, but the time for me to leave had arrived.

Editor's Note: Perhaps the reader has already noted that Ruth is now speaking of her own decisions and not talking about what the aunts and uncles of her extended Hoffmann family are telling her to do. She is her own woman. She is a liberated woman now, fully capable of making her own way in life. Ruth is happy with the refined and accomplished woman she has become. She also still has hope of meeting her "Prince Charming", getting married, having her own children and living happily ever after.

15

The Long Train Ride to California

Three days and three nights on the train to Los Angeles – Age 21
1916 – Pasadena, CA

On the evening of July 11th, 1916, Aunt Freda and Aunt Almira took me to the railroad station and put me on the train for California with an armful of lovely flowers. I had been in touch with Aunt Mary who lived in Ocean Park, CA and invited me to come out on a visit. That, evidently, is what she was doing. Uncle Dan was to meet me at the railroad station; I would be wearing a gold heart shaped stick pin. I also had one they sent to me, but never wore.

I knew Uncle Dan the minute I saw him. Forgot to mention that on the stickpin was the Lord's Prayer engraved in the smallest lettering I've ever seen.

Back to the train, no berth, breakfast served on a small table at the end of the coach, not my idea of a happy way to travel, so changed my ticket at Kansas City the first morning (pin and ticket in envelope).[26]

Figure 18 – Heart Shaped Lapel Pin With The Lord's Prayer Engraved On Back

Figure 19 – Train Ticket From St.Louis To Pasadena And Sleeper Upgrade From Kansas CIty, KS

At Topeka, Kansas, a very nice family, mother, father and two daughters got on. We immediately became good friends. The older daughter age 18 had just graduated from high school, very quiet and kept to herself most of the time while the 9-year-old and I became good friends and spent most of the time together. The family and I ate our meals at the Harvey Houses along the way. The first night we all indulged, the food so good. We all decided to eat lighter after that.

I'll never forget the good apple pie. Know I had my share. On the last morning, stopping in San Bernardino, the father bought sandwiches for all of us. It wasn't long before we reached Los Angeles. My friends on their way to a hotel in Long Beach and I to meet Uncle Dan and there he was. The trip took 3 days and 3 nights. A most enjoyable journey!

Editor's Note: While reading these Memoirs, the reader may notice that Ruth always enjoyed her travels by train – old steam engine trains had a romantic appeal to her. As mentioned above, Ruth spent many days traveling on these old trains. Family and friends may remember that Ruth had a framed photograph of an old steam engine train on the wall of her home.

---

26 *Note that Ruth is not only able to make her own decision but also pay for the added cost of this decision. She is a liberated woman now.*

16

Determined to Earn My Own Way in Life

Meeting Family in Los Angeles – Age 21
Los Angeles, CA – 1916

Though I hadn't seen Uncle Dan since he and Grandma put me on the train in St. Louis for Hagerstown 12 years earlier, he looked the same and it was good to see him. I don't remember our ride to Ocean Park but we were soon at Aunt Mary's door to meet her and cousin Walter for the first time. I may have seen Aunt Mary earlier in St. Louis when too young to remember. Anyway, it was good to see and be with them. They were very loving and welcoming. Walter was the younger of 3 sons and the only one still at home. Another son, Daniel, my cousin, lived nearby with his wife and baby where I spent a few pleasant hours. While I enjoyed my few days visit with Aunt Mary, Uncle Dan and Walter, I knew Ocean Park was not for me.

So, my next visit was with Aunt Mary's step son, Sam and his wife Lou, in South Pasadena. They were very easy going and pleasant to be with. Aunt Mary's third son, Dan lived with them. I felt very much at home with all three. Soon we were on a weekend camping trip they had planned at Big Bear Lake. There were 5 of us, Sam, Lou, Dan, cousin Hannah Anderson's husband, Hugh and myself.

It was my first experience sleeping on the ground in a tent and I, being the one single girl, had to sleep at the end of the row between Lou and the tent. I almost froze to death at night even though it was in July. Daytime was fun though, hiking and calling across the lake to the other mountain tops hearing our voice echoing back. The little chipmunks were cute and friendly, even ran up on my lap for food. Wish I had the picture taken of them.

17

Finding My First Paying Job and Room

Finding my first job and room in Pasadena – Age-21
1916 – Pasadena, CA

Home again to Sam and Lou's. They were so kind and generous in every way but I didn't wish to impose on them any longer so hied myself up to Pasadena one morning to get a job which I did at my first stop, sewing with a Mrs. Collins who had a shop in the first block north on Fair Oaks. Then on to find living quarters, again on first trip a nice room with a Mrs. Young, just two blocks south of Colorado St., only $6 a month; bed linen and all. Think I had kitchen privileges also but don't remember cooking any meals.

Soon left Mrs. Collins to sew for a Madam Jeanette whose shop was just around the corner from where I lived. A Mrs. Baker who was in the same business and lived nearby came in occasionally to have hem stitching or something done, surprised me one day by asking me if I wouldn't like to come and work for her. I was not very happy about some of the things being done where I was, so I accepted.[27]

Figure 20 – The New Ruth At 22 Years Of Age Living In Psadena, California

Remembering Ethel Connors, with whom I'd been working. She and I remained close friends and I spent many a happy hour in her home and loved her parents. Ethel and I spent many a happy Sunday hiking while the young man she was engaged to was still in the service. And when I had my long hair cut for a bob, I had a three-stemmed switch made for Ethel's mother, her hair very thin. There was a younger brother and sister in the family. The whole family the best friends ever.

It was a pleasure working for Mrs. Baker. She did lovely work and some designs and had the very best customers. We got along fine, became good friends and even took dancing lessons together. One special customer asked me to return to England with her, more or less as a companion but I had no desire as yet to leave

California. Her husband was in the ship building business so I imagine they were quite wealthy.

In the meantime, I met a trained nurse Garnett Gurney through friends of Mrs. Young. We became very good friends and were soon sharing a lovely, large front room at Dr. Foches, mother's estate – 2nd block up on N. Marengo. Lovely Birdseye maple furniture, linens and all only $13.00 per month for two. Garnett was away from home when nursing but when home we spent many pleasant hours together. One baby she took care of was Dorothy Mc Williamson's sister, Julia, who later became the well-known French chef, Julia Childs.

It was through Garnett that I met Dr. A. B. Cliff, an osteopathic doctor. The best doctor ever. Mine for at least 40 years and his nephew also an osteopath for at least 10 years. until he passed on. Never a drop of medicine all those years from them.

Also became good friends with Dr A. B.'s receptionist, Ethel Baker; later living at her home at Mrs. Forbes. I met another very friendly young woman, Lida Jane Curtin from Nebraska. She, Ethel Baker, Garnett and I became a very happy foursome, the best pals ever. The three were all about 4 or 5 years older than me, so protecting, always like older sisters; but we had lots of fun together. I wore white shoes quite often and Lida always teased about seeing my feet (Long Fellows) coming around the corner long before she saw me. It was indeed a very happy first year in California for me.

Finally, Garnett left for home, Utica, NY and soon married after that. Then Lida left for home in Nebraska. She usually only came out for the winter months. I did see her three or four visits after that, once after I had my own home and a couple of babies. She was a lovely gifted person taught dramatics, gave readings, etc. We corresponded until she passed on a few years later.

Editor's Notes: By this time Ruth had met and made many new friends in California. She was having a good time and enjoying herself. She was employed as a dress maker and earning a steady wage – enough to easily pay her own way in life. But one recurring thought kept bothering Ruth, there still was no "Prince Charming" in her life with whom she would want to spend the rest of her life and be the father of her children. Ruth held on to her "big dream", marrying a loving husband and having children of their own.

---

27 *Being asked to work for others in the sewing business was actual proof to Ruth that she was a good seamstress and knew she was able to make a good life for herself.*

18

Using My Trade Skills and Enjoying Life in Pasadena, California

Being a Seamstress with Mrs. Ethel Baker – Age 21 to 24
1916 to 1919 – Pasadena, CA

With two members of our foursome gone, Ethel asked me to come and live at her home, 48 N. Catalina St., just a couple of doors down from Colorado Street and I accepted. The family consisted of Ethel's father, Auntie, a trained nurse and a brother, Harlan. I was soon very much a part of the family and still sewing for Mrs. Baker. Harlan

Figure 21 – Relaxing On My Climb Up Mt. Wilson

was about my age, a very nice young man, full of fun and liked to play jokes on Ethel and me. We managed to get even with him once in a while. They were like sister and brother to me. Harlan worked for Standard Oil Co. Auntie was often away nursing but when home, being a very happy soul, was good company. We even slept out on the front porch one night just for a lark and that only a few feet from the front walk. That was in 1917, something one wouldn't feel safe in doing now in 1983.

The older Mr. Baker was a gentleman but a very sad one. Years earlier when they lived in the east, he had been done out of his share of business he and his brother were in together. Think it was the lumber business. He never quite recovered and seemed to lose interest in everything. Auntie and Ethel kept the home and family going and we were a family. I even made dresses for the girls and any sewing needed to be done (see pictures of girls in dresses I made – (Picture *Not Found*).

One Sunday afternoon while writing letters at the desk and alone in the house, I experienced my first earthquake. The house began to shake and quite violently so I ran out front to see what was going on – neighbors were out on the street, the trees almost flat to the ground and sidewalks moving. However, indoors seemed the safest place to be so in I went and finished my letters. Somehow or other earthquakes never bothered me much and I've been through a number of them in my 67 years in California.

Another first in 1917 was my hike up Mt. Wilson and back in one day with my good friend Edna Leonard, whom I met at Mrs. Baker's sewing shop. That was some hike, a bit too much for one day but I recovered and enjoyed many shorter hikes in the lower hills with other friends.

Still at 48 N. Catalina Street, one day I had the feeling something had happened to Father Koenitzer in Saginaw and sure enough in a letter from Mother K later, he had passed on that day.

I was sorry not to have seen Mother Koenitzer again. She was such a dear. After getting everything settled in Saginaw, she left to spend the rest of her life in Germany. At least she would be near her daughter Ella and the grandchildren she loved so much. We kept in touch, her dear letters in envelope I have saved *(Not Found)*. Ella lost her husband while he was on a business trip to the U.S. He passed on in Milwaukee, WI. Ella later came back to the U.S. visiting her aunts and relations in St. Louis. We never met but kept in touch for a while through correspondence.

Ethel loved pets, had chickens and rabbits right in the center of Pasadena. She gave me one of the baby rabbits which I named Harmony (see photograph – *Not Found*). It wasn't long however before Ethel was married to a George McCord, a very pleasant and fun person. They had been going together for some time and seemed very happy. They lived in Redondo Beach. Pasadena friends of Ethel's and I had 2 or 3 fun outings with them at the beach (see photographs – *Not Found*) swimming in the club pool, not that I swam but loved going down the big slide and managed a few strokes. Though Ethel was greatly missed, we did manage to get along at home. I did my share of housework and cooking. Harlan did his and his father's laundry (see photograph, *Not Found*). We were always happy to see Auntie home again after a nursing jaunt.

Though busy and seemingly happy, I became terribly depressed. Mrs. Baker sensed this and invited me to attend a service or meeting with her the next Sunday. The speaker was A. K. Mazumdar from India. He was a teacher and writer of religious philosophy all based on the Bible. The title of his message and writings was "The Messianic World Message". He wrote quite a few books on this subject. I attended meetings regularly and studied his messages, all very helpful and in time I was feeling much improved. I was included in an inner group who got together to talk and enjoy each other's company. Mr. Mazumdar, whom we called Prince, was always invited to join us which made the conversation so much more interesting. This was in Pasadena, then later in LA.

I almost forgot to mention another invitation received my first year in California. It was from Mrs. Fordney's sister, forgot her name, who lived in Aberdeen, Washington. She invited me to come visit her and having an interest in the steamship company, would send me a ticket. Her niece, Ersula Herman who lived with her and I had been good friends in Saginaw, MI. As much as I wanted to accept the invitation, I could not see leaving California if only for a visit. However, the next year, the sister spending a few days in L.A. and she invited me over to enjoy a lovely concert with her one evening. She was a dear person and it was so good to see her again.

Editor's Notes: Ruth said she was very pleased with the first three years in Pasadena. She was very proud of being able to earn her own living, meet and enjoy many new friends and enjoy the life she had made for herself. She and her new friends had many good times together. It also felt good to Ruth to know that other seamstresses would sometimes come to her to help them with some of their sewing projects. But there was still that inner feeling of disappointment and depression during the last several months of these three years; she still had not met her "Prince Charming". She was already 24 years old, beyond the usual marrying age and had not yet met the love of her life. Ruth said that by this time she was beginning to give up hope that she would ever meet that right man, but she still held a glimmer of hope he was yet to appear.

19

Changing My Work – Becoming a Governess

Being a children's nurse for the George Hart family – Age 23 to 24
1918 to 1919 – Pasadena, CA

About this time, still 1918, I decided to change position. I put an ad in a Los Angeles paper, to be a nurse for one or more children. I at once received an immediate reply from the George Harts, the Rosalyn Hotel people. Was interviewed and given the job. They were Christian Scientists; very nice people and they had a beautiful home. My charge was a 3 or 4-year-old boy, Bobby. He was adopted and we got along fine. He was very easy to take care of and with 2 or 3 maids in the house, I had nothing else to do. So, to keep busy did some sewing for Bobby. Even tried my hand at making him an overcoat. It was wearable (picture – *Not Found*).[28]

Another adapted member of the Hart family was Lucy, a lovely 17-year-old girl. She attended Collegiate School for young ladies. We became good friends and when possible, spent time together. Though she was used to being chauffeured everywhere, she rode down to Ocean Park with me on the street car one day just for fun; I was on my way down to visit my Aunt Mary. We walked around through the fun area and even stopped in the public ballroom and had a couple of dinners, no drinks. Then Lucy departed for home and I on to Aunt Mary's. We had fun talking about our jaunt later.

Only with the Harts, a few months and don't remember why I left, but we parted good friends. A few years later, Mr. and Mrs. Hart came to Pasadena to dine at the Huntington Hotel where I was working as a cashier. We were very happily surprised to see each other and they as friendly as ever. Later Mrs. Hart sent me pictures of all of them, taken at their new Catalina Island home (summer). Also, of Lucy, then married and with her husband Senator Hart who was George Hart's brother.

---

28 *The above paragraph is the last contained in Book 1 – Memoirs of Ruth Hoffmann Johnson. Ruth continued telling about her employment with the Hart family on the first page of Book 2 – Memoirs of Ruth Hoffmann Johnson.*

20

Finding New Inspirations at a Different Job in Los Angeles[29]

Trying a new position as clerk in a department store – Age 24 to 25
1919 to 1920 – Los Angeles, CA

While I was still in Pasadena, I took a room again with Ethel Conner's family on S. Marengo Ave. until I found a new job. It wasn't long, however, before I was employed at the Haggarty's (New York Store) in Los Angeles at 7th and Grand Avenue. A miss Carver who worked there and who attended Mazumdar's classes knew I was looking for employment and put in a good word for me. A very nice place to work and only three blocks from my apartment on 4th and Grand on what used to be called "Bunker Hill".

Everyone so pleasant and helpful at Hegarty's. I had the alteration office making appointments for fittings, etc. Also cashiering when Ada, the cashier, was not there. She and I became good friends, even took night typing classes together at one of the high schools. Ada's husband, a Dr. Brown, an MD, was very likable person. He was from Independence, MS, President Harry Truman's home town and they had attended school together. Also, on President Truman's first trip to California, the mother of our newsboy in San Marino had her photograph taken with President Truman for the newspaper. Wish I had kept it.

While at the Haggerty's New York store in Los Angeles, I became very close friends with Rhoda Mathews who worked in the credit department office. In time she became tubercular and had to give up her position. She lived with her sister Anna Schneider and Anna's husband who was the brother of Mr. Haggerty and had charge of one of the Haggarty stores on Broadway.

Figure 22 – One Of Ruth's Whimsical Creations - 1919

Rhoda also had a brother, a Dr. Tom Mathews who was head physician of a hospital in St. Ignatius, Montana where he lived. Owing to her condition, he invited Rhoda to come stay at the hospital where he could take care of her but she was not about to unless I went along with her. It was a hard decision to make since my job was my only source of income. When I mentioned this to Dr, Tom he said he'd make it good with me if I'd come along, which I did. More later.

Editor's Notes: Ruth had a very warm and loving personality. She would always "go the extra mile" to help a friend in need. She knew that her friend Rhoda, who had been diagnosed with stage four tuberculosis, wanted to spend what may be her last summer and fall at a mountain lake cabin in Montana but would not go unless her best friend, Ruth, would go with her. This was one of those difficult decisions for Ruth. Should she resign from her good job and interrupt her life goals to be a comforting companion for her best friend all through these last months of her friend's life? As you will see, Ruth chose to care for and love her friend through the last months of her friend's life, to help make these last months the most unforgettable months of her friend Rhoda's life.

Before leaving for Montana, a bit more about my life in L.A. My apartment in the Zelda Apartment Annex on the corner of 14th and Grand, on what used to be called Bunker Hill, was only 3 blocks from Haggerty's New York store, just a nice pleasant walk to work. Very friendly neighbors on either side of me. One, a Mrs. Ross, worked in the art department of the Broadway Store. It was only 2 blocks down 4th Street to Broadway; everything, shops and all so convenient at that time. Robinsons across the street from the Haggerty's, Bullocks only 2 blocks down 7th to Broadway and Barker Bothers first store only ½ block form there. Of course, that was 60 some years ago. None of those ghastly high-rise buildings of today, 1985.

All the while I was attending Mazumdar's Philosophy classes and meeting the friendliest people there. One couple, I've now forgotten their names, wanted me to come live with them. The wife a lovely person who had a beautiful voice and sang in one of the churches. The husband a very pleasant person was connected with the grain exchange in Chicago, and was away part of the time. They had a lovely home in Hollywood across the street from the old Hollywood Hotel. They invited me to dinner and a drive one Sunday, which was most enjoyable. Their invitation to come live with them was indeed very tempting and hard to turn down, but I had advice from a good source not to accept and very glad that I didn't.

Editor's Notes: Ruth said that she had already made the decision to make her own way in life and not be dependent upon someone else, at least until she found the right man, the one she wanted to be the father of her children – the one with whom she wanted to spend the rest of her life. Ruth knew that the requirements she had set for a man to become her Prince Charming were high and her high expectations may negate some men from becoming candidates. But she had made up her mind that she was only going to marry a good, capable, dependable and loving man or not get married, ever.

---

29 *This page is the beginning of Book Two of the hand written Memoirs of Ruth Hoffmann Johnson.*

21

Time Out from Work to Be with My Dear Friend, Rhoda Mathews, in Her Time of Need

Being a personal companion to my dear friend in need– Age 25
1920 – St. Ignatius, MT

Back to Rhoda – I knew she would be happier if I went with her to Montana, hoping that in time, with good care and plenty of rest, she might recover. Dr. Tom then came to L.A. by train and took us back to Montana the same way. The train ride very pleasant. We played pinochle most of the way. When we reached St. Ignatius where Dr. Tom lived, Rhoda was taken right to the hospital. It was run by Catholic Sisters (Nuns) and in connection with their church next door. Everyone there very cheerful and helpful, Rhoda in good hands.

Dr. Tom had an apartment connected to the drugstore he owned; there I had a room also. And in the drugstore, sometimes when busy, I helped, even learned to make an ice cream soda.

Cordelia, the young woman who managed the drugstore and

I took care of the apartment which included Dr. Tom's office; she had high hopes of marrying him someday. As far as I know, her dream never materialized. She was a very nice person, easy to get along with and being the doctor's ever-ready right hand, don't know what he would have done without her. Only hope he left her well taken care of when he passed on some years later.

St. Ignatius was a small town with a few stores and conveniences to suit those who lived there. Many Indians in that part of the country, mostly half breeds in town.[30]

Rhoda receiving good care in the hospital was quite happy and comfortable there. I visited her quite often, just a nice walk from the drug store.

Cordelia's family, mother, father, sister and brother lived a few miles out on a farm. All very friendly and sociable, invited us out to dinner a couple of times which was a real treat.

As soon as the weather warmed up, think it was about June (1923), Dr. Tom engaged a trained nurse for Rhoda, her name, Mercedes, who took us all up to Lake Mary Ronan. The drive was a long one through the Flathead country where lived many Indians.

When we reached the lake, there was a trim looking log cabin waiting that Dr. Tom had rented for us. It was furnished with beds, tables and stove but no convenient cupboards for our own personal things like combs, brushes, etc. So, we acquired some apple boxes with a division in the center and hung lengthwise gave us two shelves each of our own and with a pretty ruffled curtain hung from the top to cover all; looked pretty nice.[31]

Figure 23 – Typical Log Cabin At Lake Mary Roan, MT, copied from Wikipedia

Mercy, as we called the nurse, had full charge of Rhoda, while I did the cooking, etc. Our old fashioned cookstove burned wood. Mercy and I often took turns sawing or chopping some on an old tree stump out front for that purpose. When we ran short, we had to carry every drop of water for drinking, cooking *and bathing* from a well some distance away. The only hazard on that jaunt was meeting up with a rather mean looking bull that was often loose in the pasture.

Our cabin and two other cabins were built near the road and just above the lake (photographs in birch bark book – *Photographs not found.*). We had our own rowboat and when Rhoda felt well enough, packed a picnic lunch, often good fried chicken, and rowed across the lake where we spread our lunch out on a nice clearing of sand. Usually took our record player along which added to our enjoyment. A nice change and outing for the three of us.

Mercy and I often took turns tramping through the woods or a ride to town with Mr. Babcock, the hotel man; we never left Rhoda alone.

We became good friends with the Babcock's, Mr. and Mrs. and daughter Ruth, about my age. The hotel, their home with a couple of rooms to rent and also served meals. They were such kind thoughtful people, often brought us things we needed from the store or something special they had cooked or baked.

I went deer hunting up in the hills with Ruth one afternoon. Time passed very quickly and it began to get dark before we realized it. Not sure of our direction, Ruth had to call home by blowing into a shell which sounded like a horn and taken along for that purpose. They heard the call at home and answered the same way giving direction homeward and we very glad to reach there. We heard deer but never saw one that day.

Also went pheasant hunting in the woods one afternoon alone and came across a beautiful bird that I could have gotten easily but the longer I looked at it the less courage I had to shoot it, so walked away. I am glad I did.

Fishing was good at the lake, especially for rainbow trout. I either went alone or with a young man named Hobson. His brother a well-known physician in Missoula, MT. Hobie, as he was called, had taken over a homestead in the hills above the hotel when he returned from service in the Army. I had dinner in his cabin a couple of times.

Editor's Notes: When we asked Ruth if Hobie was one of the good men she was interested in, she answered, "No, Hobie was a very good, nice young man. I liked him. But I saw him only as a good friend, not the man with whom I wanted to live the rest of my life."

There were other friends there. One, a Mr. Eaton from Washington, DC. He had been in the service. Another, a lady school teacher from Missoula. Then I went up *to the fishing hole* once with Mr. Babcock. He hiked and I rode his horse and that bareback. Anyway, we made it and it was fun.

In the other two cabins lived the game warden and his wife in one, very friendly, helpful neighbors and next door to us, the cabin was occupied for a month or two by a mother and two sons. Nice boys and fun to hike with. They were about 13 and 16 years of age. We missed them when they left. Cannot remember their names.

We often heard the loons calling at night as they flew over the lake and packrats visiting us at night would wake us up rattling around or just sitting up on the window sill. We had fun with Rhoda's sister, Anna Schneider, when she came up to visit. She stayed at the hotel and I stayed with her a couple of nights. When she misplaced a comb or some small article, we'd tease her about the packrats carting it off.

One night when it was quite warm, we carried our beds (cots) out on the porch to sleep there. It stayed light until nine o'clock, so we enjoyed the evening reading and chatting. We were perfectly safe there and all three of us slept well. But did we get a surprise in the morning when we first awakened, there looking over the railing of the porch across form us was a big old moose cow. She was indeed taking in the sight. We talked to her but she soon moved on – not interested.

I'm sure Dr. Tom came up to visit us but I don't remember seeing him. His practice and the hospital kept him very busy.

Believe it or not, sometime in December before leaving the lake we gave a party in our little log cabin. We invited the Babcock's, Hobie, the game warden and his wife, also a couple of other people we'd been friendly with. Had plenty of goodies, lots of chatter and even a bit of dancing to our Victrola music. It was a very small way of showing our appreciation to our friends for all they had done for us and a fun time to remember.

It became quite chilly at the lake before leaving there and time for Rhoda to return to the hospital. The Babcock's invited me to stay for the winter, promising fun rides on the lake when frozen over, etc. But I felt it more important to return home and begin earning my living again.

However, in spite of Rhoda's condition, my reason for being there, I will always remember and am thankful for the many months outing and living in a part of the country I would not have seen otherwise. Also thankful for living as comfortably and freely as we did; enjoying the experiences that I had, even to helping chink a cabin one day; one day up in a tree with Hobie and Mr. Babcock picking apples; another time, a day's outing fishing and tramping through the woods with a very nice young man who had something to do with forestry or some state affairs, I've forgotten what. He even came to see me at Mrs. Schneider's after I returned to L.A. (pictures in the birch bark book, *Not Found*). In same book, a picture of the Babcocks with us and a couple of their friends there to bid us goodbye when we were ready to leave. (*Picture not found.*)

It was a sad parting for the three of us when we arrived in St Ignatius after the pleasant months we spent together. Rhoda in spite of her condition had had good care and was quite cheerful most of the time and easy to please. On returning to St. Ignatius, Mercy continued with her nursing, later married and lived in San Francisco (picture of Mercy and baby, *Not Found*).

Rhoda, on her return, was taken to a hospital for the tubercular in Monrovia, CA. She had good care but with no chance of recovery and passed on a year to the day she arrived there. It was a sad happening for all of us but a blessing for Rhoda.

Though some years older than me, Rhoda's sister, Anna Schneider and I remained close friends for some years after. We spent many pleasant hours together in her home or shopping and out to lunch. Her husband, a very pleasant and congenial person took us out to dinner occasionally even dancing when another friend was available. Anna made a fine appearance, always dressed in the height of fashion, having a good figure (picture, *Not Found*).

In spite of all this and Anna being a very special cook and homemaker, she and her husband parted company. Anna then took in a friend to share her home with her. Sometime later Anna became invalided and entered a home where she was taken care of. By that time, I was married and had a family but went to visit her when I could. She too finally passed on and was buried near Rhoda in Monrovia, CA.

Another good friend while living in L.A. was Rosie Darling. She was one of Mazumdar's followers, even gave talks on his philosophy and writings. She finally moved to Long beach where she had a married son and daughter. I had the pleasure of visiting her there a few times. Rosie was the cousin of the Wright brothers, Orville and Wilbur, who by the perfection of the airplane have won a place in the history of modern civilization.

Editor's Notes: Several times, Ruth told us that she always treasured the memories she had of these nearly seven months living in the mountain wilderness at Lake Mary Ronan. It was not only beautiful and exhilarating ambiance but also very rewarding to be there for her best friend Rhoda Mathews. It was also hard work sometimes, chopping the kindling, carry the wood into the cabin, and carrying all the water they needed for cooking and bathing up from the well. Ruth had also made new friends; She also saw another part of the country, beautiful mountain scenes, that she would not have seen otherwise and learned to do new things that she would not have done otherwise. This was a very rewarding and memorable time in Ruth's life.

---

30 St. Ignatius is a small town in Lake County, Montana, United States. The population was 842 at the 2010 census. The town is located on the Flathead Indian Reservation; see Wikipedia.

31 n the 1920s, apple boxes were made of thin wood veneer, not cardboard, with a center divider. just right to serve as a bathroom shelf when hung on the wall. Ruth even sewed a cloth curtain to cover to make it a little more decorative.

22

Being a Children's Governess Again

Governess for the Philip E. Thomas's two daughters – Age 25 to 31
1920 to 1926 – Pasadena, CA

Upon my return from Montana, it was back to a room at the Connors. It was home to me and like being one of the family. I needed to get back to work.

This time I decided to go back to being a children's governess so I put an ad into the newspaper. Again, had an immediate reply for my ad in the paper to take care of a child or two. It was from the Philip E. Thomas. After an interview with Mrs. Thomas, the position was mine.

The feeling for this kind of work was more or less a selfish one for I loved a nice home, surroundings and being one of a family. My charges, two little girls, Anne and Louise. Anne, about five years old and Louise about a year and one-half; both very sweet and unspoiled. I loved them both and our days were spent happily together.

The Thomas' had not been living very long in California and

were living in a very well-furnished two-story home on Bellefontaine Street, one block from Orange Grove Avenue (pictures, *Not Found*). They had a good colored cook named Booker. I knew her husband, he was the doorman at the Citizen Bank; a nice person for the job, very gentlemanly. We only lived in that home about six months.

We then moved to the Vista Del Arroyo Resort Hotel on Grand Avenue overlooking the Arroyo and Colorado Street bridge. A beautiful view! We lived at the hotel several months while their new home on California Street was being built. First rooms in the hotel then a cottage. We were treated royally. There was a special corner in the dining room for nurses and their charges but Anne and Louise were so well behaved we had our table in the main room. Coffee even brought to me out on the terrace in the afternoons when the girls were out there playing with their friends.

Mr. Steve Royce was manager and I believe owner of the Vista Del Arroyo Resort Hotel. He had a lovely family of a wife, 2 sons and a daughter. The Royce's became good friends of the Thomas', moving in the same circles of friends so I became very well acquainted with them.

Soon we moved to the new home on East California Street near Cal Tech University. The new home was lovely and very pleasingly furnished, all on one floor with a nice big screened porch in the rear. It was also furnished with table, chairs and comfy seating. The girls and I had two rooms; one, my bedroom, the other a nice big playroom. Also had our own bath room and a big screened in porch for the girl's beds. They loved sleeping out there. We had plenty of closet and cupboard space for all three of us.

At Christmas time, a large long stand or table was placed in the center of the playroom on which stood the Christmas tree surrounded by railroad tracks for their electric train. What fun it was and it added greatly to our Christmas enjoyment. The elders and guests enjoying the fun as much as the children. Mr. Thomas would come in occasionally to give the train a few runs. It was quite an amusement for all.

The Thomas's home was a pleasant one. Both parents seemingly pleased with my care of the girls. Besides outings near home, we enjoyed vacations in Santa Barbara. The first one at the El Encanto Hotel up on the hill, lovely! Later at the Mira Mar Hotel in Montecito. There we had a cottage with service from the hotel.

Another year we lived in a rented, very nicely furnished home in Santa Barbara having a maid and all. This was just a couple days after the severe earthquake Santa Barbara had in 1925, doing a terrific lot of damage in town with several blocks roped off. We felt a few jolts (aftershocks) in bed at night but no one seemed to mind.

Back to Pasadena – In time I learned to drive a car which was very necessary as Mrs. Thomas was going east to a hospital for surgery and I was to do the marketing and take the girls to school (Montessori), horseback riding lessons or whatever. Little Louise didn't care for school when she first started. She said, "If that's all we're going to do is play, I'd rather stay home." So, home she was allowed to stay for a while. They had a nice big yard to play in. One big corner of the back yard was made into a sandbox several feet long and wide with rope swings (picture) where their neighbors and school friends loved to come and play.

We often took long walks in our safe pleasant neighborhood. All quite new at that time. My car, a *1920* Cleveland, which no one now in 1984 remembers, was put out by one of the big companies and I made good use of it. Taking Anne and Louise to their horse-riding lessons near where the rose Bowl was later built and to school and other appointments. Got along fine with my driving

– it was not as hazardous as it is now. How-ever, had one slight accident which I will never understand. Was crossing Colorado Street one day, not a car in sight either way and had only gone a few feet when a fast-running Ford hit me from the left side damaging the front of the car. The driver didn't stop. I backed up my car and stopped at the corner. couldn't believe what had happened when out came the real estate man from his corner office to see if I was okay. He said he couldn't imagine where that car came from; he had been looking down the street and it was clear. After a few consoling words, he advised me to drive right to the police department and report what happened which I did. The car repaired in a short time and I on my way again.

Figure 24 – Ruth In A 1920 Cleveland

One day when grandpa and grandma Thomas were out on a visit from Johnstown, PA, I drove them back to the Huntington Resort Hotel where they were staying and I didn't quite make it to the front door landing. The doorman who always greeted and assisted guests said, "Well that's alright, you will make it the next time." Never dreamed then that someday in the near future, he would become my father-in-law. He was Harry Johnson. My future husband's father and I hadn't as yet met the son, Charles Stanley Johnson. He also worked at the hotel.

Editor's Notes: This note is to introduce the parents of Charles Stanley Johnson, the "Prince Charming" that Ruth has not yet met. Harry Charles Johnson and Anna Francis Lippincott Johnson whom I introduced above are his parents. Mr. and Mrs. Harry Johnson own a home in and were residents of Bridgeton, NJ, for the past nearly 40-plus years. Harry's normal work was as a farm laborer at various vegetable farms in Cumberland County, NJ, "the summer vegetable basket"-for-New York City and surrounding cities. But as Harry approached his 60th birthday, working as a farm laborer was becoming too painful and he was being picked fewer and fewer days and earning fewer and fewer dollars each year. Harry really needed a less physical job in his old age.

Through the summer months of 1926, Stanley Johnson, their son, had gone to Florida to work as a real estate salesman. Before returning to his job in Pasadena, CA, Stanley went to New Jersey to visit his parents. Understanding his parents' situation and since Stanley was the Service Manager at the Huntington Resort Hotel, he hired his father to be one of the "Doormen" at the Huntington Resort Hotel. He also helped his mother get a job as a maid at the hotel. Stanley then bought three tickets so that he and his parents could travel together on the train to Pasadena, CA that fall. Included as perks of their new jobs was free room and board at the hotel. Because both were earning a wage, Harry and Francis were now able to save enough money during each holiday season to live comfortably in their own home back in Bridgeton, NJ, for the rest of the year. Good fortune was shining down on the Harry and Francis Johnson family.

Ruth will tell you in her own words about who Harry and Francis

Johnson are later in her own charming story.

The grandparents from both sides of the family of Anne and Louise Thomas came out to visit while I was with the girls. Mrs. Thomas's parents, the Martindale's, came from a suburb of Pittsburgh, very quiet, reserved people and pleasing to have around. Mr. Baker, Walter, was one of Mr. Martindale's best friends. The Thomas Sr. was also very pleasant and friendly but a bit more outgoing. Their home was in Johnstown, PA, the city of disastrous floods. They like many others who could afford it had their home built high on the hill overlooking the city with elevated car service. One year they even brought their chauffeur, William, along.

Mr. Thomas Sr. owned a department store in Johnstown, PA and believe it or not, I had been in that store some years earlier when I lived in South Fork, PA when I was living with my Uncle William and family. I was sent to Johnstown a number of times on errands for my uncle. The Conemaugh River ran near the railroad station and through that area of the city. The streets usually flooded when the water was high. The railway station was built several steps up from the street; the tracks on higher ground also. When sent there one day the water had almost reached the top step so had to take the next train back home. There must have been many flooded buildings at such times.

Almost forgot to mention Sims, Thomas's black cook in their home. An older and very good person, a good cook also. She finally had to leave because of health problems. Sometime later, living with her daughter-in-law and bedridden, I went to visit her. She was so pleased. Upon leaving she said, "Ruth, you're the last good white friend I have." She passed on shortly after that.

Not very much later, I too left the Thomas's which was a sad time for me, especially leaving Anne and Louise; I had been their Governess for six years. Though I'd had plenty of time to myself and one day a week off to spend and enjoy with friends, I was in need of a change and a bit of help health wise.

I took a room with my friend Anna Schneider in Los Angeles for several weeks doctoring with a very fine well-known doctor nearby. After a thorough examination, he put me on liquids mostly – no medicines- and in time advised me to spend some time in the mountains if possible. Being my favorite place for a rest and vacation was good news to me.

Editor's Notes: Ruth loved being the governess of Anne and Louise and she loved living in the Thomas's beautiful home. She always remembered her six years working for the Thomas's as being a wonderful time. But Ruth knew that in just a few years the girls would not need her anymore. It was time to leave.

Ruth's time working for the Thomas's was during the "Roaring Twenties". It was 1926 and she was now 31 years old and never married. She was now considered by most to be an "Old Maid". Ruth was fearing what would happen to her in her old age if she did not get married now. Over the last year or so with the Thomas's, she noticed that her health and energy had begun to decline. She thought that this was due to the stress she was feeling about getting older and not knowing how she was going to support herself in her old age.

Ruth was trying to realistically understand her life's situation. She had not accumulated any life savings for her retirement years. She knew that she could make a good living through all of her work years but at this point, could she save enough money to last through her retirement years. This thought was causing much stress in her mind. Ruth felt that she needed to take some time off to rest and recreate herself. She even went to see a doctor who confirmed these thoughts.

The year is 1926. This is before the Social Security Act was enacted. The preferred way for a woman to live a respectable life in her old age in this era was to be married. Alternatively, she had to own her own business so she could make regular deposits into her own savings and retirement account. To do the latter, Ruth needed to have her own thriving business and build it up to be very desirable among the local population so that she could make regular deposits into her retirement account. If she started her own business now at this age, would she have enough years to accumulate a sizable retirement account? Whatever savings she accumulated when she reached 60 years of age would have to do. Ruth's ending thoughts about life in her retirement years were not very reassuring, hence the stress.

Even under all this stress, Ruth still believed that her best choice would be to find a gentle loving man who loved her and get married. But where should she go to have the best chance of finding this "perfect man who would sweep her off her feet". To have a reasonable chance of finding this "perfect" man, she would have to have a job where she could meet many mature, affluent bachelors. She decided to get a job at a resort hotel for a couple of years. If she did not find her man there, she would have to start her own sewing business. After telling about these times in her life, Ruth added, "I still had hope for meeting this special man, having a happy marriage and raising my own family."

23

Rest and Recreation in Big Bear Mountains

Recuperating in Big Bear Mountains – Age 31
Summer and Fall of 1926 – Big Bear Mountain, CA

It wasn't long before I was enjoying my stay in a small furnished cabin at Big Bear Lake high in the mountains. The name of the resort, Oak Knoll Lodge. It was owned by Mr. and Mrs. Augustine. We soon became good friends and there wasn't a thing they wouldn't do for one to make one's stay comfortable and enjoyable. They also had a small grocery store which was very convenient and Mr. Augustine did some baking; his coffee cakes a treat.

I had friends up a couple of times, Anna Schneider and Olga Kennedy visited me. Friendly neighbors next door, two southern girls, sisters. We hiked together and spent many pleasant hours chatting.

On the other side for several weeks lived the Pelton Motor Car Co. family, Mrs. Pelton, two children, a nurse and a cook. Mr. Pelton only came up on weekends. They were lovely sociable people and made the most of their time together, going out to dinner etc., even inviting me along a couple of times. Once in a while Mrs. Pelton and I took a short hike together, always very pleasant.

Figure 25 – One Of The Cobins Of Oak Knoll Lodge At Big Bear Lake

Occasionally the Augustine's invited their guests to sit around a bonfire outside in the evening to enjoy each other's company telling jokes and amusing stories. The latter, Mr. Augustine, was an expert with jokes. I always remember the one when his wife left him standing in the middle of the road on the hillside. The car stalled and Mr. Augustine got out to place rocks in back of the back tires so the car wouldn't slide down the hill. Mrs. Augustine then at the wheel got the car started, forgetting her husband, drove all the way home. This one always got a good laugh but we never did find out how he got home.

One was always welcome to accompany Mr. Augustine to town when he went down for supplies. There was a drugstore, beauty shop and several other mall shops there, also a Post Office.

All very convenient.

Was invited to dinner several times by Mrs. Augustine. She was a good cook and so generous. They had a little German maid who took care of the cabins, public bath and bed linens. Knowing a little German, I was able to help her with her English which she was so anxious to learn. A bit of fun on the side for me. She was such a dear person; I think possibly in her late thirties.

Had a boat ride or two earlier with a young man guest. Don't remember his name.

Towards the end of September, guests were fewer and it was quite chilly, especially at night. Had four heavy blankets on my bed then. I left the end of the month with Anna Schneider spending the last two weeks with me. Was sorry to leave the Augustine's after the many pleasant weeks spent at Oak Knoll Lodge (see photograph above) but that day arrived and off we went on the bus. This was in the fall of 1926.

Editor's Notes: Ruth always said that she really enjoyed the beauty of Big Bear Mountains and the fresh air one takes in when living up there. It was refreshing. She could think more clearly about how best to prepare for retirement in her old age. Even though she was already 31 years old and never married, she had a glimmer of hope that she could find the right eligible man to marry if she was working where some mature bachelors would be coming around. Now that she had the time to think clearly there in the high mountain air, she remembered that there were young unmarried men coming and going at the Vista Del Mar Resort Hotel; that is where the Thomas's were living when she first began to work for them. She also recalled that Mr. Stephen Royce who owned that hotel now owned the Huntington Resort Hotel in Pasadena. Ruth made the decision to write a letter to Mr. Royce to ask him for a job at his resort hotel. She wrote that letter and mailed it before leaving Big Bear Mountain that fall.

24

Back to Work: This Time at The Huntington Resort Hotel in Pasadena, CA

Earning My Own Way in Life Again – Age 31 to 32
1926 to 1927 – Pasadena, CA

Sometime before leaving the Oak Knoll Lodge at Big Bear Mountain, however, I had written Mr. Royce, who now owned and managed The Huntington Resort Hotel (now years later it is the Huntington Sheraton Hotel) in Pasadena, if he could fit me into a job at the hotel as I wished to change my occupation. He responded and after returning to Pasadena and an interview with him, was given a job as cashier. Also bonded to take care of the vaults back of me, where guests kept their valuables.

Editor's Note: When Ruth returned to her room at Anna Schneider's home in Los Angeles, a letter was waiting for her from the Huntington Resort Hotel. Ruth was invited to call and make an appointment for an interview with Mr. Stephen Royce. She made that call and was excited to see and talk to Mr. Royce again. He hired Ruth immediately and asked her to begin training that day. It was just a few weeks before Thanksgiving and soon after the Christmas Day celebrations and then the big New Year's Day celebration season. Mr. Royce needed all the good employees he could get.

Ruth was elated with the job and the people with whom she worked were great. She was now living at the hotel and the gardens all around it were beautiful. Most important, there seemed to be some mature, affluent, eligible bachelor guests walking through the lobby each day. Ruth concluded that she had made a good decision. She still had a little hope that she would someday find the right man to marry, her "Prince Charming who would sweep her off her feet, they would get married and live happily ever after".

In addition to the usual guest rooms and suites available within its main building, the Huntington Resort Hotel had many private family cottages situated around its landscaped gardens. The guests visiting the Huntington Resort Hotel were affluent corporate owners and executives with their families. Many of the guests would come for the Thanksgiving holiday and stay through to end of January or even mid-February. The families came from all around the United States of America and Canada. They would come for two reasons. The most important was to get the whole family out of the frigid weather in their home state during the holiday season and celebrate the Thanksgiving, Christmas and New Year's holidays in the warm winter climate of Southern California. For the sports fans, they would also attend the spectacle of the Rose Bowl Parade and then the famous Rose Bowl football game. Remember, there were no TV sets and television broadcasts then. If you wanted to see the Rose Parade and the Rose Bowl football game, you had to travel to Pasadena, stay overnight in one of the hotels there, get tickets and go in person.

Before I go further, wish to mention the Thomas's again, Mr. Thomas Sr. and the Martindale's, Anne's and Louise's grandparents. When they were told of my stay at Big Bear Lake and why, each sent me a nice check to help pay my expenses there. It was indeed a great help and very much appreciated. It was wonderfully kind and thoughtful of them. The best friends ever.

Back to my job at the Huntington Hotel. It was in the fall of 1926 when I started working there. I liked the job but it took time to get used to it. Every one so kind, pleasant and helpful. I had my own room, maid service and good food. I made out bills for guests upon their departure and when not sure of something or in a pinch, Margret Eckoff came to the rescue. She ran the business office and in charge of my work, money and all. She was quite pleased with what I did and we became very good friends, enjoying time out with friends.

Shortly after I came to The Huntington Resort Hotel, a very trim, nice looking, well-dressed man came in with gloves in hand, walked back of the clerk's desk, looked through the mail and appeared very much at home. Not having seen him before, I naturally wondered who he was and what right he had, taking the liberty he did. Come to find out later that he was Charles Stanley Johnson, service manager during the busy winter months. He had just returned from Florida where he had been selling real estate during the summer. His desk was across the lobby and in full view. Every once in a while, I'd catch him eyeing me, never dreaming that in time we would become good friends and I going out with him. We were married in April or May believe it was. Again, I am getting the cart before the horse.

The winter spent at The Huntington Resort Hotel was indeed very pleasant and rewarding; meeting people from everywhere. One guest, a business man from Saginaw, MI couldn't believe that I had lived there and knew Congressman Fordney and his family so well having lived across the street from them with Mother and

Father Koenitzer. Wouldn't he have been surprised had I told him that the day before I left Saginaw, Mr. Fordney said, "Ruth, if you ever want to come back here and the folks across the way are gone, you come and live with us." We were then riding down town together on a small streetcar that ran to the end of the street, Gratiot Ave. There were cars in the garage but I think Mr. Fordney just didn't want to be bothered driving. He was such a fine person, the whole family lovely.

My very best friend at the hotel was Peggy Beatty – ten years younger, a college graduate and very good company. We spent most of our spare time together. Peggy came to the hotel through her mother's acquaintance and connection with hotel people; her work also. And I believe they also came from Mr. Royce's home town in the east. Being very bright and capable, Peggy soon became Mr. Royce's private secretary.

25

Meeting and Marrying "My Prince Charming" Charles Stanley Johnson

Meeting the love of my life and marriage – Age 32 to 33
1927 to 1928 – Pasadena, CA

Until I'd met Stanley, I had more or less given up the idea of getting married, being that I was perfectly happy and satisfied with life as it was and liked my work and had plenty of good friends. However, Stanley became so attentive and lovable, couldn't resist him. Before I realized it, we were planning to get married even though he was so involved in his work at the hotel and business of his own. Being a very enterprising person, we found it difficult to plan time away. However, we finally made it; a trip to San Bernardino, just the two of us.

Editor's Note: Looking back on the many Johnson family gatherings and celebrations, I now realize the day, month and year of Ruth Hoffmann's and Charles Stanley Johnson's marriage was always a mystery, not only to their three daughters and their families but actually to all the public. All through the many years of their lives, Ruth's three daughters and their husbands were never invited to celebrate any marriage anniversary for Ruth or Stanley nor was there ever a mention of their wedding day. Ruth on the other hand was always present for the wedding anniversaries of her three girls or she sent an appropriate greeting card of the anniversary. Uncharacteristically, we, their immediate descendants, did not know in what year, month or day they were married. Nor did we ask why their marriage was not celebrated among the family just as we did for our own marriages.

Thinking back on what you have read in this book, you know all of the important vital records of each Hoffmann family member provided by Ruth throughout this book and they are accurate. But, here in this chapter where she is telling about her marriage to Stanley (a very important event in her life), there is no mention of time, date, year or place of their marriage. Why?

Now, some thirty pus years since Ruth's death, the Editor made repeated searches to find a record of Ruth's and Stanley's marriage or marriage certificate in the Los Angeles County Clerk Records. Not finding it there, they must have gotten married in one of the other neighboring counties. Then the Editor made repeated searches to find a record of Ruth's and Stanley's marriage or marriage certificate in the San Diego and San Bernardino County Clerk Records. No marriage record was found there as well. At that point, it was decided that a more thorough search should be made through Ruth's Birch Bark Scrapbook, her metal Records Box and box of photographs to find this important document. All of the family believed that they were married; there must be a marriage certificate somewhere.

We did find their marriage certificate in Ruth's treasured steel box. We now know Ruth and Stanley were married on 23 May, 1927 in the small community of Mentone, a suburb of San Bernardino, CA. We know it was a private marriage for Ruth says it was in her Memoirs, "It was just the two of us." It is also worthy of note that this marriage *certificate is again safe in Ruth's Metal Box which is in the possession of her granddaughter Karen Alexander and a digital copy of that certificate is held in the George D. Dill Family Library.*

Having spent so much time searching for and reviewing this marriage certificate, once we found and read it, several important new questions arose. They are as follows:

1. *Why did Ruth and Stanley not want their friends and the public to know that they were married? They were each mature, employed, upstanding individuals, legally and financially capable of entering into a marriage.*

2. *Why did they each not use their current home address on their application for marriage when they filed for their license with the County agent? They were both employed by and living at the Huntington Resort Hotel. The Huntington Resort Hotel is a well-respected employer and many of its employees lived in the Hotel and used its postal address as their personal postal address.*

3. *Why did both Stanley and Ruth not use their usual name and signature when they filed for their marriage license with the San Bernardino County agent? They were certainly not celebrities in hiding and they were not fugitives from the law.*

4. *Why did Stanley and Ruth choose to not celebrate the anniversary of their marriage with their three daughters and their families throughout the remainder of their lives? They*

> did have a good marriage and their marriage did produce three beautiful and wonderful daughters, 13 grandchildren and many more great grandchildren.
>
> 5. *Why did the person who performed this marriage not file their application in the normal manner with the San Bernardino County Records Office? Officially, they were never married. In fact, they were married in every way.*

None of us in the family ever posed these questions to Ruth or Stanley. These five mysteries have only been observed now after reading the actual marriage certificate, nearly 100 years after their marriage. Even though we now know of the above mysteries, we can all joyously declare that Ruth did meet and marry her "Prince Charming". Together, Ruth and Stanley birthed and raised three beautiful girls and each of their three girls lived a long happy life.

Because of so much gossip among the employees of the hotel, Stanley wanted our marriage kept secret, for a while anyway. He did tell his good friend and employer, Mr. Royce, however. A short time later, Mr. Royce invited me into the lounge for a chat. He knowing me well also told me how pleased he was that we married. He praised Stanley no end for his accomplishments and what a good man he was, etc. Of course, I already knew that but it was good to hear coming from his boss, especially Mr. Royce. He ended our pleasant chat wishing us both much happiness.

Stanley was indeed Mr. Royce's right-hand man. I have several letters he wrote Stanley through the years praising him for his help and accomplishments *(No letters found)*.

In the late spring or early summer, don't exactly remember when, I left the hotel. We rented a cottage in a court on N. Catalina

Street just a few doors up from Colorado Street (now Boulevard) in Pasadena. Stanley had lived there before with a friend and liked it for it was only a short distance from the hotel, close to good market and shops too.[22] Was in my own home at last and enjoying it.

Editor's Notes: During those first several months after her marriage to Stanley, Ruth could hardly believe she was married. She had been dreaming of this time for 30 years. She loved being married to Stanley. She said, "He continued to court me as if I was a Princess. He was indeed my 'Prince Charming'". They had also found a small cottage and moved all of their belongings into it. These were indeed special treasured days for Ruth.

The working hours for Stanley was different from most employees who had an eight-to-five job at a regular corporation. His job was Manager of Guest Services at the Huntington Resort Hotel in Pasadena. He was always dressed in a fine suit, white shirt and necktie. He had to conduct himself in a gentlemanly manner with all of the guests at the hotel and he conducted himself the same way at home with Ruth, their daughters and their families and with their friends as well.

Stanley's job required him to be present at the hotel from 8:00 AM to 8:00 PM. So that it would not be 12 hours of work each day, Stanley also had a private room at the hotel where he could rest and relax during the non-busy-hours of 1:00 PM to 5:00 PM. However, he was on call during that time if need be. Stanley reported directly to Mr. Stephen Royce, the owner of the Huntington Resort Hotel. Stanley was the person that Mr. Royce would turn to when something within the hotel needed attention. Stanley would see that whatever needed attention or repair was properly fixed and if an employee's performance was not up to par, Stanley was the one who would see that it was corrected.

Ruth said that she understood why he was at work 12 hours per day and was happy with his job. Early on in their marriage, it was established that Stanley was in charge of things at the hotel and Ruth was in charge of things at home. This arrangement of responsibilities worked well for both of them. When Stanley came home, Ruth always saw to it that he was well taken care of. She would cater to his wants and needs and he loved it. They always spent a few hours together at home each evening before going to bed and she always fixed him a good breakfast before he left for work the next morning. He knew that she loved him dearly and she would always take good care of him, their family and their home. And Ruth knew that Stanley would always have a good job which would provide for their financial needs and then some. Ruth had indeed found and married her one true love.

---

32 *Charles Stanley Johnson lived here before when he was married to Phebe E. Reeves. She died in childbirth on 19 May, 1926.*

26

Meet Our First- Child – Ruth Francis

Becoming a mother – Age 32 to 33
1927 to 1928 – Pasadena, CA

It wasn't long before we knew there was a baby on the way so I had plenty to do and to plan for.

Once in a while a friend or relatives stopped in. Also had Anne and Louise in to lunch with me, remembering the foods they enjoyed. Stanley also invited his friend Pat to dinner when he himself would be home. Pat also worked at the hotel. Think Stanley brought him along from Florida. He was a nice gray-haired older man, very pleasant. We had a thing going about biscuits – how they should be made and which one of us made the best. Just a bit of fun.

Shortly after our first Christmas and New Year – 1928 – our first baby arrived, little Ruthie, on January 3rd. It was a busy time at the hotel for Stanley. That year both holidays came on Sunday so the New Year's parade and Tournament of Roses was celebrated on Monday, January 2nd. It was a beautiful day and while hanging up a few pieces of washing on the line between the cottages, I could hear the bands playing on Colorado Street as they passed our street.

About 11:00 PM that evening had a feeling I should be on my way to the hospital. Knew Stanley wasn't available so-called Dr. Cliff's assistant who came immediately and took me to the hospital in South Pasadena where osteopaths were accepted. Stanley stopped in to see me about 2:00 AM on his way home. Baby arrived a few hours later around 6:00 AM. All went well.

And before I go further, just a bit about osteopathy. So many people are not aware of what the treatments are or what osteopathy accomplishes. Osteopaths manipulate the body, keeping it and the inner organs in shape. They do not fill one with medicine and drugs. Diet to them, is very important also. I started with Dr. A.B. Cliff in 1917. He was recommended by my nurse friend Garnett Gurney. It was there I met Ethel Baker who became a very close friend. She worked in the doctor's office. Dr. Cliff also had patients in Glendora, coming out one day a week.[33] All through the years he was my very best friend. His nephew, also a Dr. Cliff, worked with him later and took over the practice when Dr. A.B. Cliff retired. When the latter met Stanley, he was very pleased saying to me later, "Where did you meet a man like that?"

Everything having gone well for baby and me at the hospital, we were home in no time and soon doing everything that comes naturally with having a baby. Fortunately, I knew a nice woman who had worked for Mrs. Thomas when I was there and she came to do the housework for me for a while. She was a great help.

Stanley, now Daddy, had named the baby Ruth Frances so from then on, she was little Ruthie to me. She was a good baby and all went well but her feeding after a while. Cow's milk didn't seem to agree with her so doctor put her on goat's milk. It did and corrected whatever was wrong. She got me up promptly at 6:00 AM every morning for her first feeding. And she was only a very few months old when she recognized the sound of her Daddy's car coming in the driveway in back of our cottage. She would hold up her finger as if to say, "Listen, Daddy is coming." She also waved her hand back and forth keeping time to any music that she heard.

We had a nice front porch, 2 or 3 steps up from the walk next to the house. During the summer two sides of the porch were covered with vines and pretty blue morning glories. A nice protection from the walk. When it was warm enough, I sat Ruthie out there on a quilt with her toys (picture, n*ot found*). She was happy and perfectly safe there. At night when tucked in her bed, always had to have a dolly or two and a couple of animals tucked in with her

Always took Ruthie to the market with me in her lovely carriage, one that I had bought from my cousin, Walter True. Touched up and relined with beige corduroy, it was like new. At that time, I was still wearing a hat which Ruthie very much objected to so I put it on the last thing before wheeling her out. She didn't see it then and once we were on the way she didn't seem to mind.

All was going well for us when in the early fall we had a surprise, another baby on the way. The hotel business at that time of the year was rather quiet. Stanley busy only mornings and early evenings so spent the rest of the day selling real estate out at Walnut Acres in San Fernando Valley. He was never one to take it easy, always interested in some extra business.

Dad Johnson, the hotel doorman that I mentioned earlier when driving the Thomas' Cleveland car, came out bringing Mother Johnson a bit earlier that year from their home in Bridgeton, New Jersey. They were very kind, gentle people like their son Stanley. Nice to have around and they were with us quite often; Mother helping me out when necessary. Time passed very fast.

The holidays came almost before we knew it. First, Thanksgiving then Christmas and then New Year 1929. Stanley's birthday in between or near, December 16. I'm sure we celebrated all to some extent but with Stanley so busy at that time, I too do not remember. Little Ruthie not old enough to know what it was all about would be having her first birthday on January 3rd. She was almost a New Year's baby. Don't believe I baked her a cake; it would not have been good for either one of us. No doubt Mother and Dad were over to wish their granddaughter a Happy Birthday and celebrate a bit. Birthdays in those days for us did not seem to mean much with everyone so busy. Remembering, yes.

Editor's Notes: It had been nearly 20 months since Ruth and Stanley were married. So many things had happened through these months. They had moved into their own little cottage; birthed their first child, a daughter, Ruthie, was born. Stanley's parents had come out early that November from New Jersey to rejoice with them and to get acquainted with their new granddaughter. This was such a happy celebration time and scene. Ruth could hardly believe this was her new life. As she thought back to the time twelve years before when she made the courageous decisions to commit herself to make her own living and to go to California on her own, she could hardly believe she had planned such a marvelous life on her own; "This was most certainly God's plan for my life all along. Thank you, God."

---

33 *Ruth Hoffmann Johnson lived with her daughter Mary Louise Johnson Coppock in Glendora at the time this memoir was being written.*

27

Meet Our Second Child – Mary Louise

Having our Second Child – Age 33 to 34
1928 to 1929 – Pasadena, CA

Time marches on and before we knew it, it was time for our new arrival. Our 2nd baby girl born on April 15, 1929 at a small but very pleasant hospital on North Lake Street in Pasadena. Another darling baby girl that her Daddy named Mary Louise. As before, all went well for baby and me. The nurses all so cheerful and helpful, couldn't seem to do enough for us. Three mothers and babies in our room. And the food there so good. I couldn't leave at the end of the week without thanking the chef personally and he very pleased also. I'll always remember the beautiful flowers my dear friend Edna Leonard sent us at the hospital. One, a basket of the loveliest pansies. Wish my mother could have seen them, they were her favorite flower.

Soon home and everyone thankful and happy that all went well for us at the hospital. Grandma Johnson took care of Ruthie while I was gone. Mary Louise was a dear sweet baby, very quiet and easy to take care of. I do not ever remember her crying when a baby. When a little older she was quite shy. She and Ruthie, when a little older seemed to like each other very much and I know Ruthie was happy to have a baby sister.

Life went on very happily.

Mother Johnson came to take care of the girls when I had an appointment or shopping to do. She and Father Johnson spent Sundays with us when convenient and Stanley home. They departed for home in Bridgeton, NJ when the busy season was over. There they had more family. A married daughter, Ethel Weber (Stanley's sister) and her husband, Allan and their three sons; Allan, Jim and Jonathon. Also, other relatives.

We missed Mom and Dad when they were gone but occasionally a friend dropped in to see us. We also had good neighbors next door. A mother and older daughter. They were from what I call my home town, St. Louis, MO. The first and only people I've met from there in all the years (69 in 1985) I've lived in California. Anyway, we spent many pleasant hours together relating to places and areas we knew so well in St. Louis. They loved Ruthie and Mary. In the early fall they moved. We were very sorry to lose them.

Time passes on – It wasn't long before we were looking forward to Dad and Mother Johnson's return that coming fall, a lovely time of the year and cooler. Soon planning for Thanksgiving and the holidays. With all of us in good health and happy, time passed quickly. It wasn't long before we were making plans for Christmas. With cards to get, write and ready to send; some baking to do, especially cookies. And a good dinner to plan with Dad and Mom Johnson being with us. Stanley did most of the Christmas shopping for me the first year or two, what little we did. Anyway, we fared very well and enjoyed the holidays.

The girls happy with their toys and we happy to have Grandpa and Grandma Johnson with us when they could spare the time. They being our only relatives nearby, our South Pasadena cousins Sam and Lou had moved to San Fernando Valley. Dan, Aunt Mary's son with them and brother Walter and his family of wife and daughters, lived in Los Angeles. And, Aunt Mary gone before I was married. So, we were very much alone as far as family was concerned.

Now in 1985, Dan at the age of 93 is living with his daughter in San Diego. She, I understand, is in the real estate business.

I don't seem to remember a Christmas tree in our cottage that first Christmas but we enjoyed our cards from friends and relatives with their thoughtful messages. Aunt Elizabeth always sent gifts for Christmas and birthdays especially to Ruthie and Mary, as did Aunts Lillie and Freda, next door neighbors of Aunt Elizabeth and with whom I had lived in St. Louis.

Editor's Notes: It had been just over one year since they were all together, Grandma Francis, Grandpa Harry, Stanley, little Ruthie and Ruth, celebrating Ruthies first birthday. And now they were all together again celebrating Christmas and the New Year again but this time there was another person participating in this celebration, little Mary Louise, Ruth's and Stanley's second daughter was almost nine months old. Two beautiful daughters; Ruth could hardly believe her good fortune. After recalling this part of her life, she often added, "This must have been God's wonderful plan all along."

28

Meet Our Third Child – Anita Louanne and Moving into Our Own Home

Having our Third Child – Age 35 to 36
1930 to 1931 – San Marino, CA

It wasn't long before we were celebrating the New Year of 1930 and Ruthie's second birthday on January 3rd. She only two years old then and we had known for some time that the girls were going to have a baby brother or sister some months later. Our family was indeed growing and it gave us something to think about and plan for; larger living quarters for one thing.

Stanley and his parents had an interest in a house in San Marino just the right size and only a short distance from the hotel. Don't know how they worked it out financially, Stanley never wanted me to be concerned with such detail. However, it became our home. Grandfather and Grandmother Johnson didn't return home to New Jersey that summer, they stayed and helped us move and they moved in with us. What a blessing and what help they were. However, before moving in, the house inside was all done over; walls woodwork and everything. Stanley and I made a trip to Barker Brother's in L.A. and in a few hours had chosen our furniture, rugs, curtains and drapes, linens and all.

Editor's Note: Being an enterprising young man, Stanley was very knowledgeable of and constantly looking for good real estate buys. Several months before the Christmas Holidays he had looked at a single-family home for sale in San Marino during one of his mid-day breaks and was convinced that it was being undervalued; this was just after the stock market crash in 1929. At the announcement of the coming of their third child and the need for a larger home, Stanley decided that this was the home he wanted to buy for his growing family. But he did not have enough ready cash available to make the down payment. Stanley discussed his situation with his father, how this home was undervalued and it would be good for Stanley's growing family but he did not have the ready cash for a down payment.

After much discussion among Stanley and his mother and father, all three agreed that Stanley's parents would make a gift of the additional money needed for Stanley to buy this new home for his family. However, the only way Harry and Francis could acquire the cash needed was if they sold their family home in Bridgeton, New Jersey. The plan that Stanley and his parents finally agreed upon was, 1) Stanley's parents would sell their family home in Bridgeton, New Jersey immediately to their daughter Ethel and son-in-law Allan Weber, 2) Harry and Francis would make a gift of one half of the cash proceeds to their daughter Ethel and her husband Allan Weber for the down payment to buy their home, and 3) Harry and Francis would make a gift of the second half of the cash proceeds to their son Stanley and his wife Ruth for the down payment for their new home in San Marino, CA.

In a matter of a few months and the exchange of many letters and legal documents between California and New Jersey, Stanley's parents had sold their home to their daughter, received the proceeds and gifted the first half of the proceeds to their daughter, Ethel and her husband Allan, for the down payment of their new home in Bridgeton, NJ, and gifted the second half of the proceeds to Ruth and Stanley for the down payment for their new home in San Marino, CA. Stanley and Ruth immediately used their share of the proceeds to buy and remodel their new family home at 1901 Euclid Avenue, in San Marino, CA. Ruth could not believe how well things were working out for her and her growing family – soon to include three daughters.

Some other important details about Francis and Harry Johnson's financial gifts also need to be mentioned here. Stanley and his parents, Francis and Harry, soon to be the grandparents of three Johnson baby girls, would stay with Stanley and Ruth in the Johnson's new home through the entire year of 1930. They would then return to their hometown of Bridgeton, New Jersey at the beginning of summer of 1931. This plan had several practical benefits, i.e., 1) Ruth's and Stanley's three girls would get to know their grandparents better and vice-versa for the grandparents would spend most of this time living together in Ruth's and Stanley's new family home and 2) Harry and Francis Johnson could save more of their wages they would need for their retirement fund when they returned to New Jersey.

According to Stanley's and Ruth's early agreement about responsibilities for their family, it is clear here that Stanley never discussed all the details of the above transactions with Ruth. All that Ruth knew was that Stanley had worked out a real estate transaction so that they would have the cash funds available to make the down payment needed for the purchase of their own family home in San Marino.

Stanley did not tell Ruth so she was not aware that Francis and Harry had sold their home and gifted half of the money to her and Stanley. Regardless, Ruth was ecstatic at how things were working out for her family.

We moved into our new home about the first of June, 1930. Here we had a nice bedroom for Mom and Dad, one for ourselves and one for the girls. Mother helped with the house work and cooking and Dad had full charge of the yard. We all got along fine.

Somewhere along the line while we still lived in the cottage, Mary had her first birthday on April 15th and she only one year old – always so sweet and good. We loved her so.

All went well in our new home at 1901 Euclid Avenue in San Marino CA. We were happy and comfortable with more room to move around in. And it was good for Stanley to have his parents living with him for a while. Also, for the girls having their grandparents to be near them and get better acquainted for they were the only grandparents they would ever know. And they were so loving and caring.

Grandfather had fun with the girls. When Mary rode her scooter in the house, he had a cute saying like, "Skedaddle, daddle!" or something to that affect, which made her laugh and scoot faster than ever.[34] He was a very kind, gentle person which was a great help to him and his job at the hotel.

Grandma was very helpful with the girls and they loved her but things had to be done the way they were used to, especially for Ruthie. Mom told me this herself – she was fixing Ruthie's hair, believe it was when Ruthie said "No, Grandma, that's not the way Mommy does it". Not that she was hard to please but she wanted things done the way she was used to having them done.

Summer was sailing right along. It was August before we realized it and soon time for our new arrival. With all in good order, I was looking forward to it. The day soon arrived, early morning on the 17th. I called Auntie, my dear nurse friend and Aunt of friend, Ethel Roher, about 6:00 AM, also called the doctor and asked them to come quick as they could, baby was on the way. They made it but not any too soon. All went well as usual and before we knew it had another darling baby girl, the only one born at home. With my good osteopathic doctor keeping me in good shape, that and all the three births were easy.

So much to be thankful for. Dear Auntie stayed with us for a week taking care of the new baby. All was well but baby needed a name so this one I named, Anita Louanne – Anita after Mother Koenitzer's granddaughter and Louanne after Anne and Louise Thomas. Stanley had named the first two so I said, "Now it is my turn". He was very pleased that all three were girls. Some fathers, I think, would have been disappointed not to have had a son or two but not Stanley. He was much too busy and would not have had the time. However, he had boys working for him in his job and I think he was good influence for them. They learned to respect the rules or else and those who did benefitted greatly for he would do most anything for them.

Anita, like Ruthie and Mary, was a dear sweet baby. We all loved her so and like them, being a normal baby, only required the usual attention a baby needs and lots of loving.

Editor's Notes: Ruth wanted it to be clear, that she and Stanley had planned to have their children, one right after the other, since Ruth was already in her early-thirties when they were married and her doctor advised that the chance for a problem at birth was higher for would-be-mothers bearing children when the mother is in her upper thirties. Also, having the children close together would mean that the children would have someone close to their own age with whom they could play. Since it was planned that Ruth was going to be a full time Mom, they would have the best at-home care. Also, since Ruth had so much prior experience taking care of her cousins for six years, Ruth and Stanley were convinced that she would be the most capable of taking care of their three girls.

Ruth was very pleased with her current situation. She was married now for three years. Stanley was a very loving and gracious husband on whom she could depend. They now owned their own home in a beautiful neighborhood, and they had three beautiful daughters. Ruth felt that God had truly blessed her and all of her family. She was fully committed to making sure that her three girls would grow up in a loving family group; not become an orphan and have to live with and serve another family group a she did. Ruth was already hoping and praying that each of her three girls would someday find a good man to marry, have their own children and she would be able to visit and enjoy her many grandchildren.

---

34 Skedaddle is a word coined and used by Mark Twain in his book "Huckleberry Finn".

29

The Blessings of Our Girl's Grandparents

The Blessings of Our Girl's Grandparents – Age 35 to 36
1930 to 1931 – San Marino, CA

Again, I must add, what a blessing Grandmother Anna Francis and Grandfather Harry Charles Johnson were. They stayed with us until Dad Johnson had to return to his job at the hotel some time in December, nearing the busy season. They had their own room and meals there. We did indeed miss them but they came to visit when they could, especially for Christmas. Stanley (Daddy) always took time off to enjoy Christmas dinner at home.

One thing I regret very much is that I didn't take any photographs while the grandparents were with us. Especially some taken with their granddaughters. Pictures have always been so important to me too. This is something I'll never understand and always regret.

Editor's Note: During a search through the many photographs found in Ruth's photograph box, one photograph was found in an album that had the following names written in the bottom border –

"Mother J., Allen Jr., Grandmother J., and Sister". Many times, Ruth Johnson refers to her mother-in-law, Anna Francis Johnson as "Mother Johnson", hence the inscription of Mother J. The inscription of Allen Jr. is referring to Allen Weber Jr., Ethel Johnson Weber's son. The inscription Grandmother J. is referring to Mary W. Conover Johnson, the great grandmother of Ruth's three girls. Although it is not certain, it is believed that the inscription "Sister" refers to Anna's sister Lulu Lippincott. This is a great photograph in that it not only also includes the grandmother but also the Great Grandmother of Ruth's three girls.

Figure 26 – Grandmother Francis Johnson, Great Grandmother Mary Johnson, Aunt Lulu Lippincott And Allen Webber Jr.

When Dad Johnson returned to the hotel, we were without a

gardener so Stanley hired a very nice Japanese man whom he had seen working in the neighborhood. His name was Fred Kodani. He was a first-rate gardener, not only keeping it in trim but also planting flowers in season on his own. He was indeed a treasure. When interned in Arizona during the war, we, the girls and I took care of our own yard.[35] And during that time, also had a few household pieces like the refrigerator of Fred's stored in our garage.

We had a very destructive fire at that time too and never knew how it started. We lost or had ruined almost everything stored in the shed part of our garage; baby beds, trunks and all of our beautiful Christmas decorations. None of Fred's things were damaged, which I was glad of. They were stored against the back wall which I remember was not damaged.

I was awakened about 3:00 AM by noises which I got up to investigate and looking out the back window saw fire under the shed door. Stanley ran out to rescue the car and call the fire department. It wasn't long before we had a nice new garage and the only thing I was really sad about was the loss of furniture and our beautiful tree ornaments – not easy to replace.

When Fred returned from Arizona, he picked up his possessions and was so pleased that they were not damaged. He brought us a couple of special root ornamentals from Arizona, plants whose roots had been varnished and finished off for ornaments; I should have said very unusual. Fred was with us 25 to 30 years. He and his wife finally left for Japan to live there. We sure missed him. No one could have kept our place looking better than he did.

The last time we saw Dad and Mother Johnson is when they left for home the following early summer (1931), when Anita was not quite a year old. They had their own home and garden. Also, their daughter Ethel and her husband Allan and three grandchildren lived nearby.

Editor's Note: Actually, Grandma Francis and Grandpa Harry Johnson (aka, Dad and Mother Johnson) had already sold their family home in Bridgeton, NJ to their daughter Ethel and her husband Allan Weber in 1930 as noted in the previous chapter. Moreover, Ethel and Allan Weber and their two sons had already moved in and occupied the Francis and Harry Johnson family home in Bridgeton, NJ for a year by this time. This small two-bedroom home was fully occupied and there was no extra bedroom for Dad and Mother Johnson. Because Dad and Mother Johnson had only a small life savings, they decided to move into the "County Poorhouse", a local government provided housing for the poor who could not work. There they occupied a one-room efficiency apartment that included a double bed, a couple of chairs, a small kitchen sink and counter and a small bathroom. This would be their home for the following several years until Francis's death in 1935 and Harry's death in 1939.

Some years later, Mother Johnson was suffering from some inner affliction which did not seem to improve with medical care and it wasn't long before she passed on. It was a great shock to us and especially to Stanley and I know Dad Johnson must have felt so lost without her. They were so close and happy together for so many years. Poor Dad Johnson, he could have lived with his daughter Ethel and family but preferred to live alone. It must have been near the holidays for I remember Stanley sending him a good radio for his room, and nice warm underclothing for Christmas.

However, Dad Johnson didn't live very long after that. We were indeed sorry to lose him knowing we would not see him again. For him, I'm sure his passing was a blessing; sad though for the girls to lose their only grandparents before they were old enough to really know and appreciate them. But that is life, I guess.

My mother emigrated to America from Whales and I never knew any of her family. No grandparents there for me. Morgan was the family name and the only other member of the family that I heard about was my mother's brother, John. He was connected to a hospital in Sydney Australia until called back to England for some big affair, he still being a British subject (*no picture or clipping found*).[36]

The only grandparents I knew were my father's parents. My father passed on when I was four years old, in 1899. And I was only nine years old when I last saw my grandmother in 1904 when she and her son Dan, my uncle, put me on the train in St. Louis on my way to Hagerstown, MD to live with my Uncle Will, and his new wife, Aunt Amelia.

---

35 Stanley hired Fred Kodani as a gardener for their home in the winter of 1930. Fred continued to be their gardener for the next 12 years until he and his family were interned in Arizona as alien Japanese prisoners during WWII. True to Ruth's non-discriminating nature, Ruth offered room in the Johnson garage for Fred to store all of his family belongings until they were released.

36 John Morgan actually emigrated from Whales to Trinidad as a young man and lived there the remainder of his life. However, at least four of Bathsheba Morgan's other brothers did emigrate to, lived and died in Australia.

30

Life in My Own Home and Neighborhood

1901 Euclid Avenue – Age 36 to 40
1931 to 1935 – San Marino, CA

Back to our home in San Marino[37] – this still in 1931 – all was quiet and peaceful most days. Our three little daughters happy, growing and doing very well. They were not carted about on shopping tours, etc. as so many children are today. My doctor said, "Don't cart them around on the streets, they have plenty of yard to play in."

I was very fortunate; we had the best market and grocery store nearby. I knew the owner and a couple of the clerks. Oh, also knew their products well, having been at the store but did most of my marketing by phone. Always the best!

A very pleasant older man, Jim Francis, often took my order. One morning after my hello, he said, "Good morning Mrs. Johnson." I asked him how he knew who it was. He said, "I'd know your voice anywhere." and he continued, "Guess who I just took an order for – President Roosevelt's son.". One of them had recently moved to San Marino. The Roosevelt's daughter also, only lived a few blocks from us for a while.

Our mail carrier for years was also a Jim Francis. Odd, yes? A very nice man and a good friend. We always gave him a gift at Christmas time and he in turn had his daughter paint and decorate a beautiful ceramic set of sugar bowl and creamer and later when Ruthie was away at school in Santa Barbara, she wrote an occasional greeting to him on the backs of her letters to us.

Still in the early years in our home, our family life was a bit different than most. Stanley's job at the hotel kept him busy mornings and evenings, sometimes very late because of parties or some bit of doings which needed his supervision. After a good breakfast at home in the morning about 7:30 AM, we didn't see him until night unless to take us to a doctor's appointment or so. He had a room at the hotel where he could rest afternoons if he wished but usually filled in those hours with business of his own. All of his other meals were served there at the hotel so he was well taken care of. If he came home early enough, even about 9:00 or 10:00 o'clock, he would spend one hour or two with his stamp collection which was his treasured fun at home. If he had not been satisfied with his dinner at the hotel, I cooked him a small steak or something lighter. He was so easy to please.

When we got our television, that added greatly to his pleasure for he very much enjoyed westerns; they were really top shows at that time. I usually had a bit of sewing or something to do so we enjoyed the evenings together. Before television, however, we had a good radio which the girls especially enjoyed and had fun with. I must admit to listening to a couple of the old soap operas, Mr. Perkins and one or two others and the news.

When the girls were still home and Daddy home on Sundays, which was a treat for all of us, he usually had them out in the yard with him while he did a bit of tree trimming or whatever. Next door to us on one side was a vacant lot which Stanley was able to buy quite reasonably and we pleased to have it. More privacy for us and no trespassing by outsiders. He had it fenced in, cleaned up, then had several fruit trees planted; a couple of figs, a persimmon (the best ever) and a lemon. There was also an acacia tree, a tulip and other plants. And for the girls, he had high rope swing put up.

On Sunday afternoon we usually went for a drive and it was the one day we all enjoyed dinner together. And a good chance for the girls to spend some time with their dad.

On the other side of us lived the McFarland's. Their home farther back on their property and their nice big tennis court next to our driveway side where the girls, when old enough, were permitted to play. The neighbor's young people also, but not the boys unless they wore a shirt. General George Patton's aunt lived to the rear of us. We seldom saw her.

Our life did not change much with Stanley in the same position all through the years. Our days quiet, busy and peaceful. The girls busy with their own interests, drawing, etc. and still taking naps in the afternoons. My friends still stopping in to visit whenever free. Peggy Beatty and Olga Kennedy especially. Olga lived in Los Angeles so usually spent the day with us. She, Auntie Olga, to Ruthie, Mary and Anita. We spent many a happy day together and a couple of times all day at the beach.

Halloween wasn't a special day without Peggy to enjoy dinner and the evening with us. On one of these nights is when I first heard of "trick-or-treat". There was a knock on the front door and I wasn't prepared. All I had to offer the callers were mints and after they left, we found them scattered all over the porch. Thereafter, I was prepared with homemade cookies. One little boy coming back the second year said, "Oh, those good cookies again."

37 A photograph of Ruth and Stanley Johnson's family home at 1901 Euclid Avenue, San Marino, CA is shown in Figure 1 on Page 5 of this book.

31

My Three Girls Going to School – Kindergarten through Grade 4

"My Three Girls" in Grades 1 – 4 – Age 37 to 45
1935 to 1940 - Stoneman School San Marino, CA

However, time marches on and Ruthie was nearing school age. She would soon be attending Stoneman School which consisted of a kindergarten and four grades. Not quite sure but when she was five years old, going on six the following January, is when she entered kindergarten. Her Daddy didn't want her taken in the school bus and I didn't have a say, so had one of his boys from the hotel drive her to school (picture of Mary and Anita waiting at the gate with Ruthie) wondering, I guess, what it was all about. Ruthie left for school that morning as if it was the thing to do and got along fine at school. Sometime later, Mary, Anita and I paid kindergarten a visit which gave them a chance to see where Ruthie spent each morning.

A sad thing happened though before Mary started school; we

had an earthquake. Think it was the one in 1933 that did so much damage in Long beach. The kindergarten was damaged to the extent of having to be closed for some time and Mary missed out there. She started school in the first grade the next year and had learned so much from Ruthie that she spent only one-half term there and only ½ year behind Ruthie. A year later, Anita started school, the kindergarten had been restored and so she had the pleasure of starting there and I know she enjoyed it. All three girls got along well at Stoneman. I visited school two or three times each year feeling it was the thing to do. The teachers always so friendly and cordial.

Figure 27 – Ruthie's First Day Of School With Sisters Mary And Anita Looking On

It wasn't long before all three had their share of school and neighborhood friends. The latter playing hide-and-go-seek with the girls in the early evenings. Our lot being a perfect place to hide.

Across the street from us lived the Bragoniers. A very nice family from whom we bought our piano, a baby grand. Mrs. Bragonier had been a concert pianist and her three or four brothers, musicians with the Los Angeles Philharmonic Orchestra. They moved finally and I was sorry to see them leave.

Another very good neighbor and friend was Lucile Buck. She had two fine sons about the girls age, Dick (Richard) and Charles. Dick loved to come over and play on our piano even though he had one at home. Later he became a very fine pianist, playing for a club he belonged to up north. The boys, good friends of the girls and pleasant company. Charles was in one of our weddings, Anita's, I think. Both with good education became professors, Charles at Fullerton in California and Dick at Chapel Hill, NC. Both married and had families. We attended their weddings. Later Dick visiting his mother, came out with her to visit us here at Mary's and Chuck's. It was so good to see them. Mary and I enjoyed a couple of visits and pleasant luncheons with Lucille in her home after I moved away from San Marino. Lucille is the dear friend who gave me the baby blanket pattern from which I have had the pleasure of knitting many for family and others.

Mr. and Mrs. Church, daughter Jan and son Danny lived next door to the Buck's. Mr. Church, a busy man, we didn't see very often but Mrs. church was present, nearly a daily visitor; often 2 or 3 times a day needing advice or just for a visit. She seemed very unsettled. Son Danny, I saw very little of. think he left home quite early and was living in Pasadena. Daughter Jan was a dear and good friend of the girls and always welcome in our home. She married one of the Yeakel brother's sons. Always think of her on her birthday, May 30th.

On the other side of our lot from time to time lived two or three families. One family, the Regan's, with a couple sons, very nice people. Then the Robinsons with three sons, Matt, Jim and Eugene, more the age of our girls and very nice friendly boys. The young people all had fun together even to playing with a box of toys and building blocks on our shaded front porch on hot afternoons.

The Robinson house was two stories high and from one of the windows the boys strung a wire or cord across the lot down to the girl's side window on which they passed notes back and forth. A bit of extra fun, Yes? One of the boys, think it was Jim, on a trip to San Francisco, won a chance to call someone long distance by phone; guess who he called – this old granny. I indeed felt very flattered. Remember him sitting in the kitchen with me a couple of times when busy there. I met Mrs. Robinson but never became very well acquainted with her. Think she worked and was busy most of the time. The boys were indeed missed when they moved.

Then along came the McNeil's, same house. Mr. and Mrs., son Jack the oldest and two daughters, Colleen and Laura Ann, the latter quite small and very sweet. In later years, or some years later I should say, Colleen, a very attractive young lady, became "California Maid of Cotton". Jack was a fine boy and a good friend of the girls. We became good friends with the whole family. Mr. McNeil, a very pleasant person was connected with a bank in Los Angeles. Mrs. McNeil (Lillian) and I became good friends and neighbors, later working at Red Cross. After a few years residing next door, they moved to a new home in San Marino where we enjoyed a couple of very pleasant afternoons. After they had finished school, all three children married and had families. After Mr. McNeil passed on, Lillian moved up north to Walnut Creek to be close to some of her family. We're still friends and she planned to visit us next time she is down this way.

With so many boys living on our long block, Mary especially, had fun playing football in the street with them. Euclid Avenue, not being a thoroughfare was quite free of traffic.

Two or three other boys lived down the street. One, a John Taylor, who became a very good friend of Ruthie. For a while, Ruthie had a not-so-close school friend, Joanne Maxwell, a member of a well-thought-of family who also lived on our block. Mr. Maxwell, a lovely person whom I met at a number of school affairs.

All during this time we were still enjoying Sunday with Daddy. He had bought several acres of property in San Fernando Valley and had wonderful plans drawn for a home, café, etc. where we would live and have a business. The place was going to look more like a park - beautifully planted with a stream flowing through it etc. But the plans didn't materialize. I was sorry for Stanley that they didn't but the girls and I were very happy to stay in San Marino. Stanley still owned the property so turned it into a trailer park which then was becoming very popular. He hired a very nice couple to manage and take care of the place – still keeping his position at the hotel. So out there we drove every Sunday for quite a while enjoying a picnic lunch and "Daddy's Day" with him.

Also, the girls were still taking piano lessons which they started a short time after we bought the piano. Their Daddy was bent on them taking lessons and I very pleased. He became acquainted with a Mr. Purvis-Smith, an Englishman and a fine piano instructor. His wife also a teacher. As I remember, Stanley got acquainted with the Purvis-Smiths through Mr. Royce, whose daughter, I believe it was, was taking lessons from them.

The girls took lessons for a long time becoming very good

pianists, even playing in public, being a member of the Tuesday Musical Juniors, also over radio (Ruth and Mary). It took a lot of practicing. I sat with them for an hour or so the first year or two, helping when I could.

The Purvis-Smiths liked the girls and we became very good friends. Mr. Purvis-Smith was very interested in photography and took lovely photographs of the girls. He also did some work for National Geographic. His father was a doctor and had as a patient, Sun Yat-sen, president of People's Republic of China for a short time.[38]

One day Stanley brought a big beautiful macaw home. It had been given to Mr. Royce at the hotel. It was kept out in the gardens but was neglected by those in charge of feeding and taking care of it. When Stanley made him aware of this, he asked Stanley to take care of Polly, so Stanley brought him home. We kept him in the living room for quite some time on a two tray stand with a perch, no cage. He looked very pretty there in the corner near the window and never bothered anyone until one day when I was alone and busy at the sink in the kitchen, he came to the dining room door back of me and said, "Hello." It surprised me for a moment but then got him upon the broom handle and back on his perch.

Figure 28 – Ruth And Her Three Girls With The Parrot Outside.

He was quite heavy so I think he just lost his balance when he fell. It wasn't long before he was comfortably housed in his outdoor home. Stanley had a large wooden box placed in the corner well protected with a perch and all where he could easily get down in his yard. He was well screened in top and sides with gate and all. He seemed quite happy there and I'm sure he liked the fresh air. His speech consisted of about three words; hello, what and where. Often wondered if he had spent some time in a fire or police station.

Somewhere along the line, I felt that the girls should be attending Sunday school though Stanley and I didn't belong to any church. I had attended different ones and I liked "All Saints Episcopal Church" the best. So, Stanley agreed that's where they should go. I attended church at the same time and Stanley very happy to take us. The girls got along very well there. We also had them Christened at All Saints Church. After attending Sunday school there for a year or two, they asked to make the change to one in San Marino, closer to their friends, I think.

My mother was an Episcopalian and a very good woman. After marrying into the Hoffmann family, she attended their churches, even the German services for she had learned to understand and she spoke German. That was mostly at my Uncle Will's church. Other members of the family in St. Louis attended Lutheran or Presbyterian churches. Like Grandpa's church, Uncle Will's was an Evangelical Lutheran.

Just in case someone wonders how we managed to get around since I didn't have a car, we called the yellow cab (Tanner's) when Daddy couldn't take us. Much cheaper in those days and less expensive than driving a car. The girls did a lot of walking when old enough to be out on their own. Sorry about that, but walking was good for them. And the streetcar, later bus, was only two blocks away. When Anita was older and babysitting, she bought her own bicycle,

Editor's Note: Although Ruth does not mention it, somewhere between the years of 1937 to 1938, her Aunt Elizabeth Mellies and Aunt Louise Jürgen's came from St. Louis, MO to Santa Monica, CA by train to visit with their sister Mary Bleibtreu and her family plus their niece Ruth Johnson and her family. We know this because Ruth saved a photograph of her two Aunts that includes Ruth's youngest daughter, Anita Johnson. It was also noted that this photograph was taken at their hotel in Santa Monica, CA.

Figure 29 – Ruth's Aunt Elizabeth Mellies and Aunt Louise Jurgens with Ruth's daughter Anita Johnson

---

38 *A military uprising on Oct. 10, 1911, in Wuchang, China, marked the start of the Xin Hai Revolution. Sun Yat-sen led the Xin Hai Revolution that ended more than 2,000 years of imperial rule in China. On Jan. 1, 1912, Sun Yat-sen became provisional president of the Republic of China.*

32

My Three Girls Growing Up – Grades 5 Through 8

"My Three Girls" Growing UP- Age 45 to 49
1940 to 1944 – San Marino, CA

The girls left Stoneman School for the Huntington School on Huntington Drive, 5th to 8th grade as most San Marino children did. The school bus stopped only a couple of doors above us on our street. All three got along very well at Huntington School. They usually liked their teachers and especially Mr. White, the music instructor. He was liked by all. In fact, one of the school buildings was named after him. He also conducted San Marino's Easter Sunrise Service in Lacy Park in which the three girls sang in their Glee Club. I attended the service and it was lovely.

Lacy Park was also a very special place for picnics and family gatherings. We enjoyed a couple of our own, Daddy joining us in one which I'm always so pleased to remember.

Figure 30 – Johnson Family Picnic at Lacy Park - 1963

Editor's Notes: This was a beautiful sunny day for Ruth and Stanley with all three of their daughters and their families at Lacy Park in San Marino, CA. Those present at this picnic are:

1st Row: Charles Gordon, Karen Dill, Louise Coppock, Lisa Dill, James Dill

2nd Row: Bill and Paul Gordon, Terry, Mary and Chris Coppock, Chip Gordon

3rd Row: Stanley and Ruth Johnson, Hugh Gordon holding Ruth Ann, Chuck Coppock, George and Anita Dill.

George's Uncle John Thomas Dill was taking the photo.

I always attended PTA meetings and did my share of preparing for any special occasion or outing especially for Easter vacation week spent at the beach. Housing rented for those who could go and always in charge of a couple of the mothers. First getting together to plan and provide what was needed in the way of food, etc. The girls and their schoolmates always looked forward to this outing and I know enjoyed every minute at the beach.

The girls each had their own friends and interests. Anita joined Girl Scouts and attended for a while but don't think their activities appealed to her so she gave it up. She loved animals and 2 or 3 times brought home stray dogs that were wandering around on the school grounds. They usually ended up in the pound. Later she had beautiful St. Bernard dogs of her own (pictures) and belonged to a St. Bernard Club, also attended quite a few dog-shows with them.

Figure 31 – Anita With Ricky - 1944

Think I already mentioned our 2 dogs, Ricky and Brownie (pictures). We loved them and they were both with us about 13 years. Ricky was so cute, every time she heard the cookie jar lid, she made a B-line for the kitchen.

The girls had ducks for a while. Anita had one that would follow her up the street. I had canaries for several years and with our parrot (the Macaw picture) think we had our share of animals. Oh, I almost forgot Anita had rats for a while, one especially quite tame and had the freedom of the house – stored some of his goodies in one of Anita's dresser drawers and under a shirt in the porch closet. Henry, his name, grey and white and a very nice pet.

Back to school – Three of the boys living in San Marino and attending at the same schools with the girls became well known some years later. All three interested in politics concerning their state of California and country. They were John Rousselet, a friend of Ruth's, his office now in Washington, DC. Pete Schabarum, a good friend of Mary's who is now in 1985 and has been for some time, Los Angeles County Supervisor of the 1st District which includes Glendora. His office in L.A. The 3rd one Pete McClusky who was a senator up north later in California.

All three of the girls got along well at Huntington School. I think their happiest school days were spent at Huntington. They belonged to the Glee Club and there was dancing at the gym every Friday afternoon *with* some of their friends no doubt lifelong friends now, quite a few years later. Mary and her good friends still gather at the home of one of the girls in San Marino every two or three years to keep up their friendship and interest in each other.

Back to school – Each of the girls in turn graduated from Huntington School. Graduation day was always an exciting one. San Marino had not as yet built their high school so Huntington graduates went to what was then called San Marino and South

Pasadena High School in South Pasadena. It was at that time rated 4th highest in academics in the United States. 9th grade, Jr. High was in a separate building. A school on Fair Oaks Ave which they attended the first year. Mary was secretary of her class and on the Safety Committee.

Each in turn on their way to the main school for 3 more years. They were busy years for the girls and all went well as far as I know or can remember. It seems so long ago. I'm sure there is much I've forgotten. But I do remember speaking to the Dean of Girls, Miss Olt, one day asking how they were getting along in school. Her answer was, "Oh, they're getting along very well, they will always have their fun." and that I am sure of.

I don't think Anita will mind me adding this bit. This still at Huntington School, she recalled recently when we were talking about school that owing to the fact that we never went on vacations, Daddy always too busy, she never had anything of special interest or exciting to write for her essay when returning to school. But this one year, 7th grade, she wrote about our garage burning down – very sad – but exciting enough at 3 o'clock in the morning, fire engines and all.

One year when Anita's teacher, Miss Wicket, returned from her vacation in Hawaii, Anita had made a lovely lei with our sweet peas for her. I'm sure she loved it. Thanks to Fred our good gardener, he knew how to grow them.

33

My Three Girls in High School – Grades 9 Through 12

"My Three Girls" Growing UP- Age 49 to 53
1944 to 1948 – South Pasadena – San Marino, CA

All three of the girls were active in Blue Bonnets doing their bit to help at the Children's Hospital. Mary and Ruth also belonged to the Huntington Auxiliary, Jr. and I'm sure did their bit there with the others. The girls were seldom deprived of outings or invitations to spend time with their friends.

My three girls did their share around the house as well, even helping to do the yard work during WWII. when Fred was not here. They also earned their own pen money by babysitting and Mary also worked up at the corner bakery for a while. Then later on, all three worked at a shop or two in Pasadena. And when Bullocks opened their new store here, Ruthie worked in the collegiate department as some of her school friends did. Mary worked at Bullocks while still in high school and became a personal shopper for customers throughout the store. It was indeed a lovely place to work. Mary also did some modeling for the Adrian Modeling Agency.

Mary Coppock's Notes: Each of the three Johnson girls had their own distinct personality and character and they each had their own friends in school. Ruthie was the openly friendly one, an extrovert and the outgoing sister. She was particularly concerned about the cloths she wore and how her hair was styled, including putting many pin curls in her hair every night through her high school and college years. Mary was also openly friendly but more reserved and was equally content to spend time doing her coloring or painting on her own or going out with her friends. Anita was the introvert of the family. She was quiet and shy with those outside the family. She grew up taking good care of her dolls and the many pets she acquired all through her school and adult years.

All three of Ruth's daughters did well socially and academically at the South Pasadena-San Marino High School and they each enjoyed many school friends and their own chosen extracurricular activities.

Figure 32 – Ruth Francis Johnson - South Pasadena -San Marino High School Senior Photograph - 1946

One of Ruthie's friends and classmates, Babs Bagman, was crowned Queen for the 1945 football season and Ruthie chosen *to be one of the Princesses of the Rose Parade Queen's Court.*

Editor's Notes: Ruthie continued her education for one year at The University of Santa Barbarbra. before she returned home to be closer to her boy friend Hugh Gordon, one of her high school class mates. Ruthie and Hugh were soon married

Figure 33 – Mary Louise Johnson - South Pasadena -San Marino High School - Class Of 1946

Mary, also, was chosen Princess when her friend and classmate Susan Kemp was crowned Queen for their high school's 1946 football season and the 1947 *Rose Bowl Parade Queen's Court*.

Editor's Notes: After graduation from high school, Mary entered the Art Center College of Design then located on Third Street in down town Los Angeles. Although it was quite a commute each day, Mary attended classes there for three years. Mary met her future husband, Chuck Coppock while attending Art Center College of Design. They were married in 1951. Mary then attended Pasadena Junior College taking secretarial classes with her sister Anita as a means to earn a regular salary that she and her new husband would be able to have their own apartment and eventually buy their own home.

All the while Anita was attending high school, she was taking good care of her St. Bernard dogs. She had three of them at different times and attended dog shows with them. They were beautiful, loveable dogs and good pets. We often allowed them in the house but one did a bit of nibbling on things like shoes which was not so good. Aside from their size, they were easy to have around.

Figure 34 – Anita Louanne Johnson - South Pasadena -San Marino High School - Class Of 1948

Mary Coppock's Notes: As a small child, Anita loved her dolls and took good care of each one, dressing them properly for the day, putting each one to bed every night, etc. She loved all of our pet animals in a similar way. Later on, while in high school, Anita worked for a veterinarian in Pasadena for a short time. That is probably where she "fell in love" with the beautiful St. Bernard dogs. That may be where she acquired the large framed lithograph of a St. Bernard dog that she hung in her bedroom. One by one, she raised three gorgeous puppies there at her home during her four years in high school.

Editor's Notes: Anita continued to live at home and pursue her training and showing of her St. Bernard dogs for two years after graduating from high school. At this point she decided she needed to own her own car instead of depending on family and friends for transportation. To achieve this freedom, she decided she would enroll and complete the two years of study required to earn a Secretarial Associate of Arts Diploma at Pasadena Junior College. Having successfully completed her Associates Degree, Anita was hired as a secretary at the offices of the U.S. General Service Administration Office located in Pasadena in 1951.

Figure 35 – Anita With Her Beautiful St. Bernard Dog

Soon after she began her employment, her supervisor informed her that consistent with all US Government employee programs, she would be awarded a one-week paid vacation. This was an intriguing new idea to Anita. To use this one-week paid vacation as she really wanted, she would also need to own her own automobile. Anita now had a new goal.

All through her first year of fulltime employment, Anita lived at home and saved most of her earnings. She was determined to purchase her own automobile without taking out a loan. Anita also planned a one-week holiday at a hotel in South Lake Tahoe, CA for her mother and herself. For Anita, this vacation was a great learning experience about how to plan and do new things for herself. It was also a great joy for Ruth to see her youngest daughter bloom from child to adult as well as see the sights of another famous resort in California. Here are photographs of Ruth and her daughter Anita enjoying the beach at Lake Tahoe during the summer of 1952.

Figure 36 – Ruth At Lake Tahoe

Figure 37 – Anita At Lake Tahoe

34

Last Will and Testament of Mrs. Ruth Hoffmann Johnson

My last wishes. – Age 89
November 1984, Glendora, CA

To my family and whomever else this may concern:

If at any time I have a heart attack or whatever, please do not have me put on a life saving device or whatever. Please let me pass on. I do not want any expensive hospital bills run up to save my life or burden my family. They have all done so much for me through the years and my last few years spent with Mary and Chuck have been a blessing and I am very thankful to them for all they've done for me.

It is a pleasant thought to know that my remains and Daddy's will be taken care of by the Neptune Society.

The money in Home Savings and anything left in my Bank of America checking account is Mary's and Chuck's. Hopefully, there will be some left over after the Neptune function. It's a good feeling to know that all will be taken care of so peacefully.

However, I'm sorry that all didn't turn out as I had planned with the money. I wanted to at least leave each of my three daughters a thousand dollars apiece and had just about made it when my first eye operation was done. It cost me around $2,400. Fortunately, the second one only around $400.00. Quite a difference (a change in Medicare affairs) otherwise could not have had it done. I am very thankful to Dr. Lemely for my good sight but I'm still sorry it changed my money plans.

Concerning family possessions, they were never an issue in our home as far as I know. Everything we had was the best but no real valuables. My three daughters, Ruth, Mary and Anita, have been wonderful about everything concerning the home and what their father left for us. Everyone got what they wanted or could use as far as I know. As for the money, there was no great amount left. I still had the property and a number of things to settle finally. This in 1962 after Daddy passed on. I lived in our home another year and a half and when ready to sell there were several repairs that needed to be done to the house. Also, property value was very low at that time but I couldn't afford to keep it nor did I receive what it was worth. Did my best! Had asked in different directions for help or advice but none was forthcoming.

Presume I should have gone to work so it was a toss-up for me – either work or being free to visit and help my families when convenient. Also, I would have had to give up my volunteer Red Cross work which I thoroughly enjoyed. Daddy always so pleased to drive me there when he was still with us. He wouldn't let me get a job or work otherwise.

Daddy's business affairs were in the hands of the law office of Ross, Woodson, Millard and Woolverton which included the ranch also and for which I received a very small amount. When all was settled, the charge was $500.00 which I paid. Miss Woodson and I were good friends. She also held an office in Pasadena Red Cross. Think she was treasurer.

Back to possessions in my room: Ruthie has asked for my mother's album cover which Chuck so beautifully mounted. Also, the knick-knack frame with shelves for small ornaments that hangs over the bookcase. And in the middle drawer of my dresser is a white leather jewelry case with some jewelry she might like to have. That includes the grandchildren's pendant she gave to me and which I've enjoyed wearing and had many compliments on. I hope she never needs to sell it but Ruthie has an inlaid living room table from home which I understand she can sell for $1,000.00 in New Zealand where she lives.

For Anita and George, my Governor Winthrop desk goes with the secretary (book case and desk) from home. Also, the lovely picture of my parents and self, hanging over my desk which they so thoughtfully had mounted for me. Have already given Anita my diamond ring she always loved rings.

Anything else in pictures or whatever, Mary, Anita and Ruth can choose between them. My picture albums should go to the girls whose family pictures they contain. If duplicates of what they have, they can keep them for their grandchildren.

Mary and Chuck have Daddy's rocking chair which Chuck has kept in such good shape, recovering it 2 or 3 times. Also, a dining chair and bookcase from home. Hope they keep these. Everything else of mine, *they can* do with as they please.

Wish I could have left all something of real value. Love and good wishes to all.

Mom

P.S. Forgot to mention – Daddy's picture over the chest is for

Mary. Also, my platinum wedding ring, my granddaughter Karen Wright may have if she still wishes it. She asked for it when still in her teens – with love. Grandma.

35

Epilogue

Written by George D. Dill, Editor
2019 – 2021, Granite Bay, CA

Ruth Hoffmann Johnson was born to Agathon and Bathsheba (Grace) Morgan Hoffmann on 30 March, 1895 in Mt. Olive, IL. She lived a long and colorful life of 94 years filled with many personal relationships she developed and cherished, the many trials and tribulations she experienced and overcame, the fine foods she cooked and shared, the many memorable places to which she traveled and lived and the ever-so-many delightful and tragic events she witnessed and recalled in her Memoirs. She lived a remarkable and accomplished life.

Ruth died on 3 December, 1989 in Encinitas, San Diego County, CA content with a life well lived. At the time of her death, Ruth was living with her second daughter Mary Coppock. Mary called to gather each of her sisters for funeral services to be held as soon as Ruthie could make it to California from New Zealand where she lived. The funeral services were prepared by the Neptune Society. Afterwards, they cremated the body and placed her ashes alongside her husband Charles Stanley Johnson ashes as prearranged and their ashes were scattered together at sea off the coast of Southern California.

While "her three girls" were gathered in Encinitas to support one another during this time of grief over the loss of their dear Mother, they decided that they must do two important things. One was to properly celebrate the life that their beloved mother lived. Second, they wanted to execute Ruth's holographic will just as it was written. The Editor believes that Ruth would say of this last scene, "My three girls did all of these things well."

Sadly for "her three girls," the curtain was drawn on Ruth's well lived life more than 30 years ago. It is well past the time that Ruth's remarkable life should be revealed to all of her descendants and to the descendants of her many friends. She lived a life that gave love, hope and charity to all of her family as well as to her many friends who lived in many parts of these United States of America and now in this 21st century some live in places all around the world!

May God bless Ruth Hoffmann Johnson.

36

My Fond Memories of Grandma Ruth (GiGi) – Cherished Moments Remembered by Ruth's Grandchildren and Great Grandchildren

Quotes Collected 2019 – 2020
California, Maryland, Montana, New Zealand,
Oregon, and Virginia

This book is filled with loving memories that Ruth Hoffmann Johnson had of family, friends, acquaintances and things that occurred throughout her life. It is especially fitting and interesting to hear and communicate some fond memories her own grandchildren and great grandchildren have of Ruth. An effort was made to get as many of Ruth's descendants who knew her to write down their memories of their mother, grandmother and great grandmother.

These independent memoirs of Ruth included in this chapter

were written by her descendants 30 some years after her death. Each one may seem trivial to another but they are lasting memories to each of the authors.

Fond Memories of My Grandma Ruth
by
Christopher Coppock, Grandson

My fondest memory of Grandma Johnson was when she spent the first summer in Wyoming with us as Dad built our house and the rest of us including Grandma cleared the acre lot.

We also took a trip up to lake Mary Ronan Montana with Grandma and spent several days at a lodge where she and the friend she traveled with stayed. She always wanted to go out on the lake and row to the other side like she and her friend did. I volunteered to row and we went out several times. I think it brought back fond memories for her. She really enjoyed it and told me about those times and what they did. She said they would make fried chicken picnic lunches. She really enjoyed that trip.

- - ◇ - -

Fond Memories of My Grandma Ruth
by
James K. Dill, Grandson

Every memory of GG is a fond one. My earliest memory of Grandma Ruth is when I was five or six years old and we got to visit her and Grandpa Stanley in Pasadena. There was a huge grandfather clock with a smiling sun face, fruit trees in the yard, and a huge red and blue Macaw on a perch.

My fondest memory is when she came to visit us in Santa Clara. GG and Mom took me shopping in San Jose to a large department store, possibly Macy's. The three of us had lunch and I had a hamburger with french-fries and a root beer. I believe the ladies had club sandwiches and coffee. It might have been the most wonderful meal I ever ate.

On another visit, she bought me a banana split, which I ate, all three scoops of chocolate, vanilla, and strawberry ice cream, whipped cream and toppings. That remains my favorite desert.

Grandma Ruth never judged. She was a wonderful, smiling presence in our lives, giving love and hope for the future. She is greatly missed.

-- ◇ --

Fond Memories of My Grandma Ruth
by
Dianna Gordon, Granddaughter

I have so many wonderful, treasured memories of Grandma Ruth, too many to mention them all. But the things that stand out the most for me is how loving and kind she was. I loved to stay with her at her apartment in Pasadena when I was a child and looked forward with delight to her visiting our family home in Springville, CA.

Grandma Ruth always found the time to read my favorite stories and never hesitated give me a hug and say "I love you."

In later years, there were the fun card games or playing scrabble with her. Or sometimes, just sitting together quietly and talking. I absolutely adored her and couldn't have wished for a better Grandmother.

- - ◇ - -

Fond Memories of My Grandma Ruth
by
Lisa Dill, Granddaughter

My fondest moment with Grandma Ruth was walking down the streets of Pasadena with her. She was my world when we were by ourselves. It must have been around Christmas maybe, although it was warm. But we went to the then "Five and Dime Store" and Macy's. We must have also gone to Woolworths where the air smelled like popcorn and bubblegum all mixed up together. We had so much fun.

Then once at her house after shopping, I played outside on a sea of clover. So green and shady under the big trees. But overall, walking downtown with Grandma Ruth was the best. I couldn't ask for more.

-- ◇ --

Fond Memories of My GG
by
Erin Spring Dill Heaton, Great Granddaughter

My favorite memory of GiGi, was her and I playing Tri-Ominos at Grandma Anita's kitchen table when I was a little girl. She was always so sweet and gentle until she set up the triangle pieces and prepared to win!

Even on a sunny day, GiGi would offer me her warm sweater to keep me warm and safe. I always looked forward to seeing my Great Grandmother. She was caring, considerate and fun.

Figure 38 – Erin Enjoying Lap time With Great Grandma Ruth (GiGi)

- - ◇ - -

Fond Memories of My Grandma Ruth
by
Terry Dwiers, Granddaughter

As a child my best memories, especially of Wyoming, were of Grandma Ruth coming up to visit; picking her up in Jackson Hole and having her help us get settled in the home my dad built for us. She was out there with the rest of us, clearing our big property of weeds and brush and working very hard. In addition, I often visited her in many places she lived; her apt. in Pasadena for one.

I would go and stay with her; she cooked the most awesome meals and would sprinkle baby powder on my sheets & pillow before I went to sleep, so it smelled so nice! When I was still very young, I remember her home in San Marino and the Sunday dinners; along with playing with my brother & sister in their large backyard. My Mother gave me a lot of letters that I had written to her during the years that she must have kept; it was so nice to read them again. She always wrote me back too.

Then as the years went by and she lived in Glendora with my parents, I would visit her often; a lot of times I would go in her room and we would talk for hours, drinking coffee and catching up on life as we knew it. She was always so pleasant and fun to be with; so caring and curious to know what I was up to.

I loved hearing her stories of her past and all her memories. She was the best grandmother anyone could have and I miss her dearly.

- - ◇ - -

Fond Memories of My Grandma Ruth
by
Charles Gordon, Grandson

My earliest memories of Grandma are at the house on Euclid Ave in San Marino, CA that she and Stanley owned. Grandma would be in the kitchen with wonderful smells coming out into the living room. I would be sitting on the scratchy horse hair couch in the afternoons watching something like the Lone Ranger or an early cartoon. Something yummy would be coming my way.

I also particularly loved the walled courtyard out the front door. When it was hot, I would go out into the courtyard that was covered by the big mock-orange (*pittosporum tobira)* tree. It was lovely and soft and cool as I ran my small hand through the mossy brick edges.

Grandma was so kind and would come visit us in Springville on the ranch. I asked her once when I was very young why she had moved so far away. She laughed and said, "I didn't move so far away, you did." and gave me a big hug.

When I was older, I told her how much I loved her clock, the chimes were so pleasant to listen to. After we moved to New Zealand and on a return journey that my mother Ruth made, the clock arrived back with her. The clock now sits in our living room, telling us what time it is in the middle of the night and reminding me of Grandma and her life many, many years ago.

- - ◇ - -

Figure 39 – Charlie enjoying one of Grandma Ruth's visits with the Gordon family in Springville

Fond Memories of My Grandma Ruth
by
Louise Collins, Granddaughter

I remember being able to talk to Grandma Johnson about anything and she would listen with an open heart and no judgements. She was very sweet and caring towards everyone and had quite the sense of humor too. I really enjoyed getting letters from her when I was a little girl. She was a very special grandma.

-- ◇ --

Fond Memories of My Grandma Ruth
by
Karen Dill Alexander, Granddaughter

I have always loved gardenias and their fragrance. Grandma smelled like gardenias. She wore a perfume called Jungle Gardenia by Tovache,

I can only imagine what I said to Grandma about her engagement and wedding ring, but I am so thankful she gave them to me. As a child, they were the most beautiful rings I ever saw!

Figure 40 – Grandma Ruth is the honored guest at Karen's wedding.

There's a country western song, "I Hear Voices", about the things that people have said to us which reside within us. I hear her words often! As a 'try hard' person, often like a fish trying to swim upstream, I remember Grandma telling me to "Rest" and

"Do not always try so hard". Similarly, the Bible says, "Be still and know that I am God." Psalm 46:10. I rest in her words and this verse, often.

-- ◇ --

Fond Memories of My GiGi
by
Dawn L. Dore'

Like most family members, I have many memories of my Great Grandma GiGi, although I was very young at the time, and am very sad to not have known her in my adult years. A couple memories come to mind;

I always thought her of such a classy lady. Always dressed her best, with her broaches and scarves and her hair right in place. I remember taking her with my Nana Coppock to the salon in downtown Glendora and picking her up and excited to see what her hair was going to look like! GiGi always had a little tissue tucked inside of her sleeve on the inside of her wrist, *just* in case she needed one (and I do the same to this day!!) I remember loved receiving letters I the mail from her. She would write me so often and as a child, I was always so excited to receive mail. Her writing was so beautiful, no matter what age she was.

Her room, when she lived with my grandparents Chuck and Mary in Glendora was towards the front of the house. We would sit in her room for hours, playing with my sisters and my cousin Lacy, doing puzzles. She didn't mind us kids (quiet as we *tried* to be) playing on the floor of her room. The stained-glass hummingbirds sparkling in her window, the little coffee table full of beautiful violet's, and she would have me touch the 'fuzzy' leaves of the plants and be very careful with them. When I see anything to do with hummingbirds or violets, I automatically think of her. I love the smell of Gardenia, it is my favorite scent, and often not easy to find, but I know that she loved them as well.

I was sitting on her bedroom floor when I remember feeling my first (large) earthquake ever, but somehow felt safe in her beautiful room and she kept us quite calm.

When we'd leave my grandparents' house, she and my Nana Coppock would stand at her bedroom window facing the driveway and wave goodbye, and then draw the shape of a heart with her fingertips, and I would do it back through the car window. My Nana Coppock and I still trace the heart upon our goodbyes to this day, some 30+ years later. GiGi was a beautiful spirit and created such a beautiful family. I love and miss her dearly~

-- ◇ --

Fond Memoir of Grandma Ruth
by
George D. Dill, Son-in-Law

Perhaps the most remarkable memories I have of Ruth is her exuberance for life; in particular, a life lived with love of God, love of her family and love of her many friends and neighbors. She was ever present and helpful to each of us whenever we needed help.

One can clearly see this wonderful personal attribute when we read her words describing her memories of her father and mother. Ruth enjoyed a great relationship with each of her parents.

When orphaned as a young child of eight years, she eagerly prepared herself to help provide loving care for her twin brothers hoping that it would convince one of her Hoffmann families to take the three of them into their family upon seeing her good loving care for her brothers.

In future years, she happily served as a governess for her cousins and other family's children through many years of her young life and both the children and their parents were all blessed by her caring love and service to these many children.

Ruth lovingly fulfilled a need for a surrogate daughter to Johanne and Robert Koenitzer. Ruth lived with them in Saginaw, MI for five years. Her genuine love for them is clearly expressed in her own words here within this book.

When her best friend Rhoda Mathews was diagnosed with terminal tuberculosis, Ruth interrupted her life plans to accompany Rhoda for an eight-month farewell trip to enjoy the beauty and majesty of the mountain country near St. Ignatius, Montana.

It is also evident in her Memoirs that Ruth was loved by each of the families for whom she served as governess and she loved each of them. This was true even though the six years she served as governess for her Uncle Will's and Aunt Amelia's children were very trying and difficult years for Ruth. She continued to express her love for them many years after they last saw one another and as well as in her correspondence with them via mail.

Ruth held a true love for each member of her immediate and extended family. Everyone could observe this love each time she came to visit one of her daughters and their family or we went to visit her. This special love was also extended to some of her many friends. There was no mistaking the love Ruth placed upon us. Thank you, Ruth!

I would like to relate another fond memory of Ruth. It has to do with the contrast of the persona she presented to all in her normal everyday life versus her persona when she played the game of dominos – specifically, the game of "Sniff" dominos.

In her everyday activities, Ruth was always humble, warm and loving and used proper protocol in her relationships with others. She was never aggressive towards others, so much so that she often assented to another's wishes. She always conducted herself as a gracious matriarch of the early 20th century world.

But there was one exception to Ruth's congenial persona. She loved to play games with her children and grandchildren. When anyone played dominos with Ruth, there was an obvious change in her persona. She was exceptionally good at the game. She often won. While observing her across the table during a dominos game, she never changed her facial expression; she put on her "poker face", she played to win and never exposed what she was about to play. She knew the game very well; well enough to masterfully execute both offensive and defensive strategies that would give her an advantage.

As soon as she sat down to play, Ruth seemed to instantly change from the warm, loving, demure Grandmother that always used proper protocol in her relationships with others into an aggressive athlete intent on winning her game. Who would have believed that this "Little Old Lady from Pasadena" could be such a formidable opponent? True to her basic nature though, Ruth was always forthright and polite in all verbal intercourse with her opponents, even in the heat of the game.

Ruth was a remarkable woman, wife, mother, grandmother and friend. We have all missed being with you during the past several decades. Thank you, Ruth, for being you! May God graciously bless you!

- - ◇ - -

37

Our Hoffmann-Morgan and Johnson-Lippincott Family Trees

Researched, composed and edited by George D. Dill
2019 – 2021
Granite Bay CA

In Chapter 1 of this book, Ruth provided an accurate but limited profile of her Hoffmann-Morgan ancestors that she personally lived with and knew. She learned of these two generations of ancestors as a young child through firsthand conversations with her parents, her aunts and uncles and her paternal grandparents. The Editor has researched and presents in this last chapter, four generations of our Hoffmann-Morgan ancestors in words and in a family tree drawing. It begins with Ruth Hoffmann Johnson's generation and includes the three generations that came before her.

Although Ruth did not include any ancestral information of the Charles Stanley Johnson family ancestors in her Memoirs, the Editor also provides a four generation Johnson-Lippincott family tree. It is hoped that having family trees for both sides of our family here in one place, in printed form will be helpful to all of Ruth's descendants as well as the descendants of her friends.

It is important to credit the various sources of information used to draw each the two family trees presented herein. It is notable that Ruth gave me, the Editor, some of the family tree information directly during our many personal visits and conversations. She also gave me six pages of family tree documents about fifty years ago which I kept in my family files.

Over the past several years, the Editor used the Internet to search, collect and preserve specific public records and documents available at FamilySearch.org and Ancestry.com to verify the two family trees presented herein. He also searched selected archives located in the former country and state of residence of Ruth's and Stanley's ancestors to collect and preserve other information not currently available in Family Search and Ancestry.

The Editor also contacted and collaborated with other distant members of the Hoffmann-Morgan and Johnson-Lippincott family lines as well as other semi-professional genealogists who generously donated their expertise to some documents needed for this effort. Specifically, the Editor wishes to thank Bud Pickett who is a direct descendant of Ruth's Aunt Mary Hoffmann Bleibtreu for his contributions. The Editor wishes to thank Lori Mellies whose husband is a direct descendant of Ruth's Aunt Elizabeth Hoffmann Mellies for her contributions. The Editor also wishes to thank Margaret Scudds, who is a direct descendant of Elizabeth Morgan, Ruth's maternal grandmother, for her contributions. We all owe great thanks to these distant cousins for their contributions and insight into the Hoffmann-Morgan Family Tree provided below.

The Editor also wants to acknowledge the research and contributions of documents provided by Bill Saunderlin, who lives in New Jersey near Stanley Johnson's home town. His contributions and help to complete and verify the Johnson-Lippincott Family Tree presented herein. We all owe our thanks to him as well.

After the publishing of this book, the Editor plans to continue to research the lives of each of the individuals listed in the Hoffmann-Morgan Family Tree and the Johnson-Lippincott Family Tree. One important question of our Hoffmann-Morgan Family Tree yet to be discovered is, "Who was the father of Bathsheba (Grace) Morgan and who were his ancestors?"

Another important area of further research is to learn more about the life, marriage and times of Leopold Hoffmann and Elisabeth Döör, the parents of Ruth's paternal grandfather. The fact that they are the parents of Julius Hoffmann has now been verified.

As more people choose to discover their DNA and add that information to the several DNA data bases now evolving on the Internet, it is expected that a DNA match will appear someday and we may be able to learn who Ruth's maternal grandfather was and then who her other family ancestors were.

With a continuing research effort by our family and others, more distant generations of the Hoffmann-Morgan Family Tree and the Johnson-Lippincott Family Tree will become known. This information may then be entered into our respective family trees and included in future editions of this book.

The Editor invites each of the great grandchildren of Ruth Hoffmann Johnson to consider using the blank family tree pages contained here in this chapter to draw their own family tree. If you are a great grandchild of Ruth, print your name on the line at the top right branch of the first blank family tree. If you are married enter your husband/wife's name on the line at the top left of this blank family tree. And, if you have children, print their names in the space between yours and your spouse's names. Note: it is good to include each individual's birth year along with their names.

On the next rung down on this family tree, print the names of your own parent's family group that is on the right-hand side of this page. Again, print the father's name on top and the mother's name just below the family group line and the names of all of your siblings in the space between your parent's names. The names of your spouse's family group should be printed on the family group on the same branch level on the left side of this page.

Finally, enter both sets of your grandparent's family groups. To do this, print your grandfather's name on the bottom right family group and your grandmother's name just below the line of that family group. The grandmother's name to be listed here should be one of three daughters of Ruth. Then print your parents name plus his/her siblings in the space between your grandparents. Next, do the same for your spouse's two sets of grandparents.

Copies of the vital records, photographs and other family information collected that verify the accuracy of both the Hoffmann-Morgan Family Tree and the Johnson-Lippincott Family Tree are preserved within the George D. Dill Family Library and are available for perusing by family members.

The Editor invites all who read this book, if you find any family information, stories or documents not included in this book, please pass that information on to the Editor. It will be held in the George D. Dill Family Library and included in later editions of this book.

Hoffmann-Morgan Family Tree

- Ruth (3/30/1895-12/3/1989)
- Wilhelm (12/21/1903-5/27/1904)[1]
- Frederick (12/21/1903-2/18/1904)[2]
  - 1st Agathon Hoffmann (1869-1899)
  - 2nd William Hoffmann (1874-1917)
    - Julius Hoffmann (1833-1899)
      - Leopold Hoffmann (1805-1875)
      - Elisabeth Döör
    - Louisa S. Kemmerich (1836-1905)
      - Andreas Kemmerich (1797-1860)
      - Erdmuthe (1830)
    - Siblings of Agathon/William:
      - Mary M. (1860)
      - Daniel (1862)
      - Elizabeth (1864)
      - Margarethe (1866)
      - Charles (1867)
      - Agathon (1869)
      - William (1874)
      - Paulus (1876)
      - Martha (1878)
      - Johanne (1878)
      - Louise (1881)
      - Julius (1883)
    - Julius Hoffmann siblings: Johann A. (1822), Andreas C (1825), Marie W. (1827), Andreas G (1833), Louisa S. (1836)
    - Louisa S. Kemmerich mother: Johanne S. Schwab (1801-1861)
    - Father(s) Unknown
  - Bathsheba Grace Morgan (1868-1903)
    - Benjamin (1862) Charles (1865) Bathsheba (1868)
    - John A. (1848) Thomas (1851) Martin (1854) William (1859)
    - Elizabeth Morgan (1827-1910)
      - Unknown
      - Unknown
    - Thomas Morgan (1788-1865)
      - Benjamin (1823) Elizabeth (1827) John (1829)
      - Elizabeth Reece (1787-1864)

Treasured Legacy

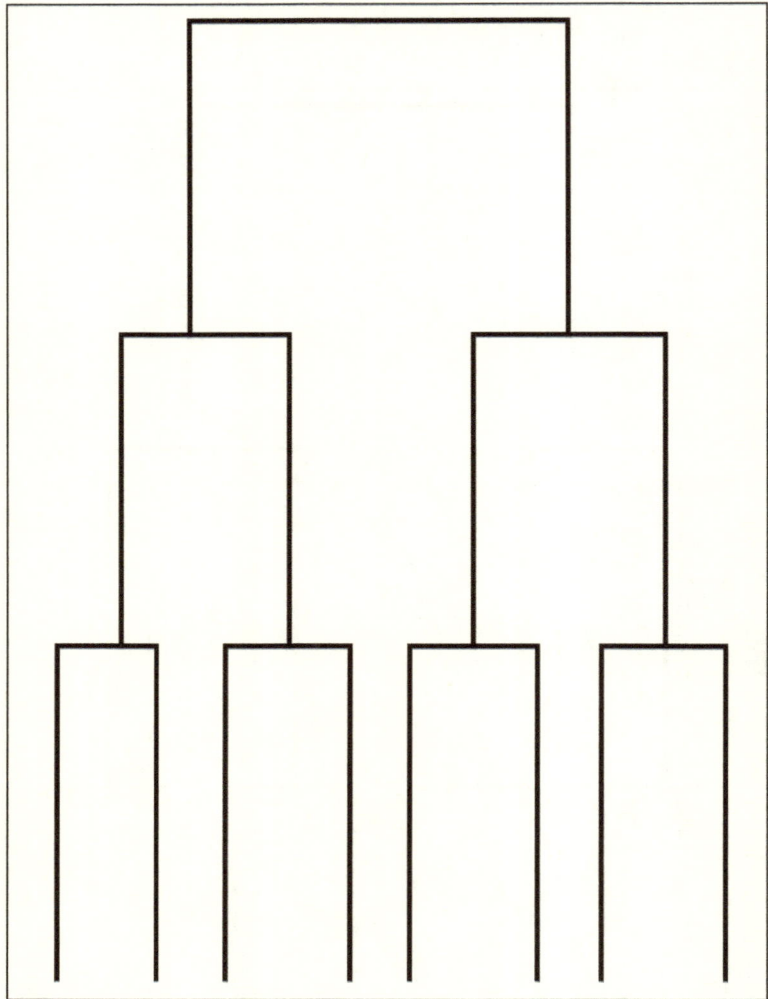

Johnson-Lippincott Family Tree

- Harry C. Johnson (1868-1907)
  - William A. Johnson (1839-1907)
    - Daniel Johnson (1795-1847)
      - Elizabeth (1817) Joseph (1821)
      - Danial (1824) Martha (1826)
      - Sarah (28) Roulef (31) George (34)
    - William (1839) Margaret (1841)
  - Mary W. Conover (1842-1920)
    - Peter Clark Conover (1828-1895)
      - Sarah Green (1850-1915)
      - Elizabeth (1838) Mary W. (1841)
      - Hannah(44) Sarah(46) Daniel (48)
      - Harriet (1851) Caroline (1854)
      - James (56) John (59) Clark (64)
    - Sarah Fish Boroughs (1820-1898)
    - Thomas Lippincott (1790-1865)
- Charles Stanley (1892-1962)
- Ethel M. (1895-1993)
- Anna F. Lippincott (1872-1938)
  - Isaac Lippincott (1835-1885)
    - John (1822) Joseph (1826)
    - Thomas (1828) Abigail (1830)
    - Danial (33) Isaac (36) Anna (38)
    - Rebecca (1840) Elizabeth (1844)
    - Ann Stanger (186-1888)
    - James Simnerman (1819-1896)
  - Abigail A. Simnerman (1840-1920)
    - Abigail (1840) Anna R. (1842)
    - Charles F. (1844) Levi (1847)
    - Caleb F. (1849) Alonzo (1858)
    - Letitia Albertson (1820-1881)

Children:
- James (1862)
- Harry Charles (1868)
- William H. (1874)
- Herbert Locke (1879)
- Albertus (1885)
- Letitia A. (1869)
- Anna Francis (1872)
- Lulu H. (1878)

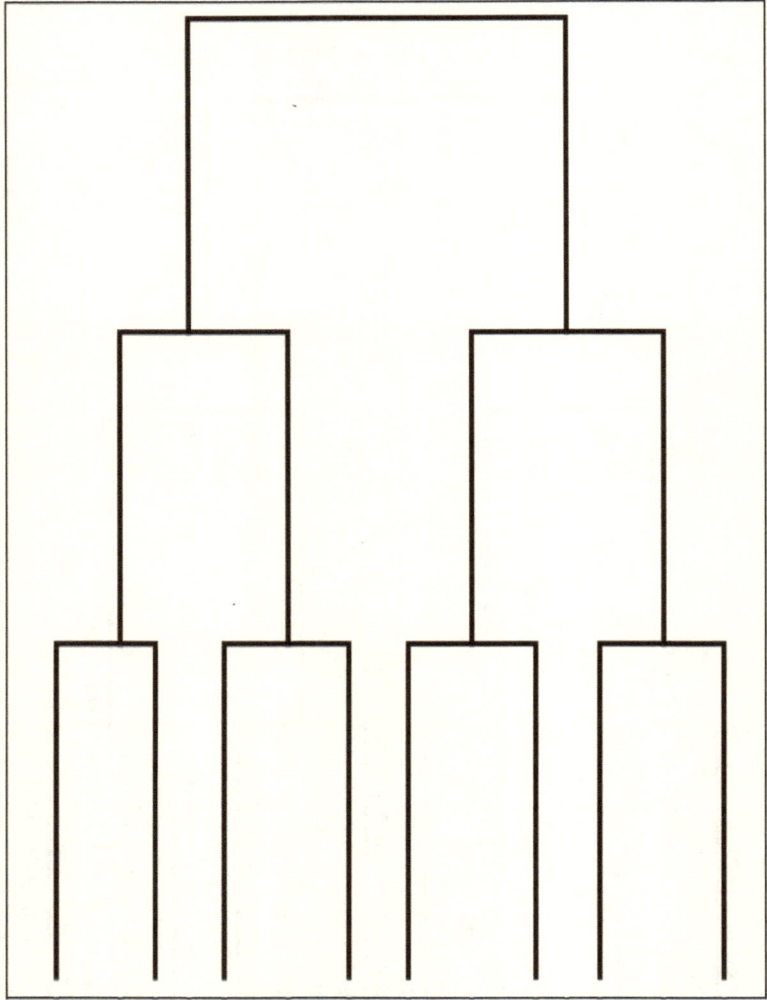

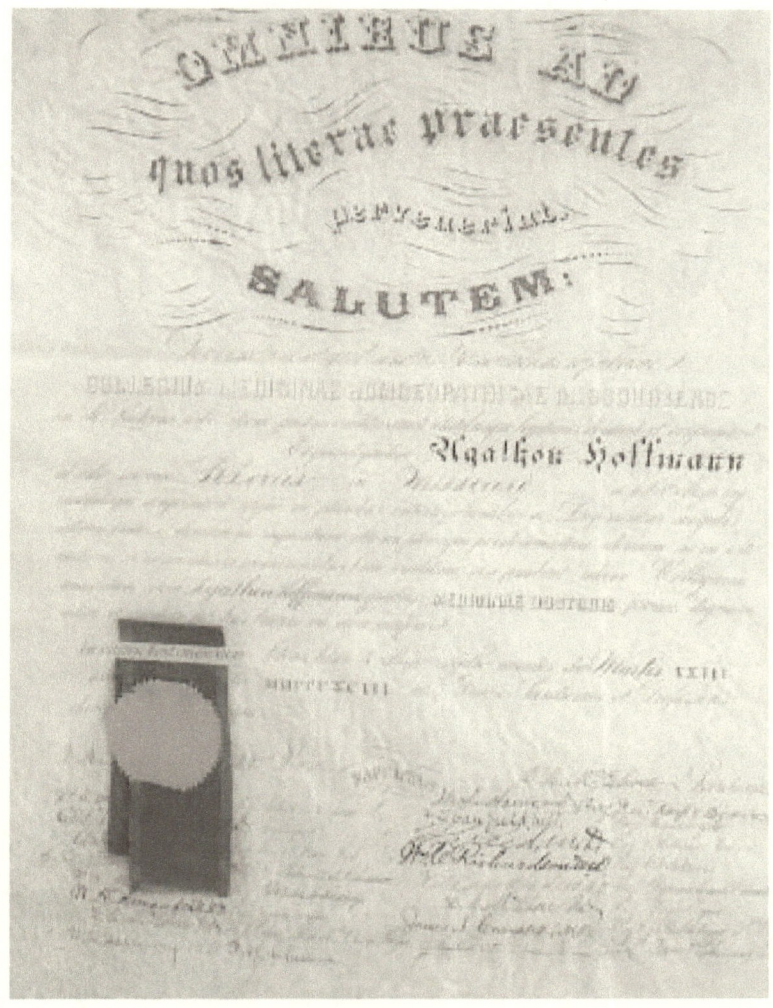

Attachment 1 – Photograph of Agathon Hoffmann's - Doctor of Homeopathic Medicine Diploma

www.ingramcontent.com/pod-product-compliance
Lightning Source LLC
Chambersburg PA
CBHW020905080526
44589CB00011B/452